Doc Eifrig's Retirement Solution

HIGH INCOME RETIREMENT

How to Safely Earn 12% to 20%
Income Streams on Your Savings

By Dr. David Eifrig
with Brian Hunt

Published by Stansberry & Associates Investment Research.

CONTENTS

ACKNOWLEDGEMENTS

There are many people in my life to whom I owe thanks.

My path – from a small Minnesota college... to an MBA at one of the country's top schools... to a career at Goldman Sachs... and then medical school in North Carolina – was filled with wise people who laughed with me and encouraged me to do "my thing." I can't list all the teachers and instructors who patiently helped me, the golfing buddies who let me take Mulligans, or the business partners who let me ride along with their dreams. On the journey, I always seemed to have enough of whatever I needed. I suspect it was because of the many people who shared themselves with me along the way.

Two special people on this trip helped me pretend to be a writer. I suspect if you pushed them they'd confess to doing much of the heavy lifting.

The first guy, Carli Flippen, has been masterful as my "managing editor." This is the person who helps writers meet deadlines with leads and paragraphs that keep the reader interested. He prevented me from stumbling over my writing like a puppy with a basketball. To you Carli, cheers. I hope we can continue the journey for another decade. And if you agree, I'll keep sharing wine from my stash.

The second guy, Brian Hunt, is the true force behind this book. Side by side, we hatched the idea two years ago on a sunny bench outside the Orlando Money Show. It took hours of rewriting, editing, and a little bit of screaming on my part. It took tons of discipline and laughter on Brian's part. Late in the process, he reminded me that he didn't need credit. He does. Thank you, Brian Hunt, for your help and friendship, but especially for your dogged determination to see this book through my hands.

To these two guys and the many others at Stansberry & Associates who helped launch this into orbit and get out the word on what I think is one of the most interesting topics of investing – options – here's to your health, wealth, and a happy retirement.

– Dr. David Eifrig, Jr.

FOREWORD

On June 2, 2010, Dr. David Eifrig began an extraordinary scientific demonstration.

This demonstration lasted several years. It changed the lives of thousands of people for the better. The demonstration covered several powerful investment techniques that few people have ever heard of... and even fewer understand.

It produced a set of investment results that – although verified by specialist lawyers – is still controversial... and to some people is "too good to be true."

For those who participated in his demonstration, nothing about it is "too good to be true." The money is in their accounts. And for most, it was a life-changing event... one that is helping them safely extract millions of dollars from the stock market.

Even as you read this, thousands of regular folks –

schoolteachers, plumbers, veterans, nurses, and housewives – are using these hidden techniques to make hundreds, thousands, <u>even tens of thousands</u> of dollars a month.

In this book, you'll hear their stories... you'll discover how these hidden techniques work... and you'll learn how you can immediately put them to work to create huge income streams from your investment portfolio.

But before we get into these stories and techniques, we need to shatter a big investment myth...

This myth prevents older folks from enjoying the retirement they expected. It costs them:

- Nice dinners
- Better vacations
- Leisure activities
- Years of early retirement

The myth is that it's impossible to earn large amounts of investment income on your savings without taking big risks.

This idea – which you'll hear from many financial advisors and brokers – is simply wrong.

Right now, as you read this book, it's possible to earn 12%-20% yields a year on your money – safely.

This is not a joke.

It's no wild marketing claim.

It's 100% real.

You see, when you start out in the stock market, you're told that an annual dividend of 3%-4% is a satisfactory yield on your money.

And as for bond investing, in today's era of low interest rates, most folks are ecstatic to earn a 3%-4% annual interest yield on their bonds.

But when you learn Doc Eifrig's techniques, you'll realize it's possible to earn much greater yields, very safely. You'll see that you can earn 3%, 4%, or even 5% yields not in a year... *but in just three months.*

That's right... What most "regular" people wait 12 months to earn, people who learn these techniques regularly earn in just three months. Looked at another way, they make the same amount of investment income in just 25% of the time... and without tying up as much money.

Again, let's be clear, these folks earn giant yields without taking big risks.

I've discovered that for many folks, learning these techniques is a revelation. It's like having a blindfold lifted from their eyes.

Just take the story of Justin E., who wrote to Dr. Eifrig:

"I love your work!... It has certainly changed my investing style and my life. So far I am up 40% this year."

In the pages that follow, you'll learn everything you need to know in order to join the small – but growing – number of people who are generating the safest double-digit retirement yields anywhere in the world...

THE CONTROVERSIAL TRUE STORY OF GOING '136 FOR 136'

Stay on a financial website for more than a minute, and you're bound to come across some wild marketing claims.

You'll see investment "gurus" claiming gold is set to triple in value. You'll see analysts gushing over the next "miracle cure" cancer drug... and the gains investors stand to make. You'll see people touting the latest "green" technology that will bring oil companies to their knees.

These financial marketing claims – like any marketing claim for any product – are carefully constructed to catch your eye.

They're often outrageous.

They're often unbelievable.

And they often get folks interested in research, products, and services that fail to live up to the hype.

This is a big reason why Dr. Eifrig's "demonstration" stirred up so much controversy... and so much excitement.

Using the techniques you'll learn in this book, Dr. Eifrig – in a live demonstration that ran more than three years – **closed out 136 consecutive trading positions for a profit.**

That's not a typo. That's 136 consecutive trading positions closed for a profit.

We hope you're extremely skeptical of that claim. You should be.

I've been in the investment game for around 15 years now. I've worked with, met, or read pretty much every star "investment guru" in the world. I've tried just about every investment and trading strategy under the sun. I've lost and made hundreds of thousands of dollars. And I know how marketers can "massage" numbers in order to make claims that mask the real performance of investment strategies, tools, and vehicles.

Thus, I'm what you'd call an "extreme skeptic."

And I can tell you this "extreme skeptic" wouldn't believe the "136 for 136" claim if I hadn't seen it with my own eyes.

I wouldn't believe it if I hadn't watched this strategy direct thousands of dollars in regular income payments into my brokerage account. I wouldn't believe it if we didn't have so many excited readers writing to us every week about how the service is changing their lives.

Still, Doc's demonstration generated a lot of controversy.

Many of our readers literally don't believe anyone could close 136 straight winning positions. As I mentioned, I'm glad those people are skeptical. In today's world, you can get taken for everything you have if you're not.

But in the case of Doc's demonstration, the claims are real.

That's why he has developed what you could call a "cult following" among American investors. Right now, these "cult members" are earning safe, 12%-20% yields on their retirement accounts.

They're doing it by mastering one of the safest, most powerful – and misunderstood – financial tools on the planet: stock options.

Here's his incredible story...

     - Brian Hunt
     Editor in Chief
     Stansberry & Associates Investment Research

136 CONSECUTIVE WINNING POSITIONS: THE *RETIREMENT TRADER* STORY

— 1 —

It was hard to walk away from another million dollars.

I began my Wall Street career in 1984. But before going to business school, I'd already dabbled in a few stocks during my college days. I made big money on the merger of packaged vegetable brand Green Giant into Pillsbury and then lost it all on a solar-energy stock based out of Colorado.

I had already seen a lot of ups and downs in the markets before graduating from Northwestern University's Kellogg School of Management with my newly minted MBA. My start at Goldman Sachs was exciting. Back then, a million dollars was a stupendous – almost unimaginable – amount of money to me.

But in 1994, after 10 years of working for a couple of the world's elite banks as a "derivatives" specialist, I walked away from a job that paid me hundreds of thousands of dollars... including year-end bonuses of seven figures.

But don't get me wrong, I was no disgruntled "whistleblower." I had a great time on Wall Street. But I wanted more out of life than expensive suits, fancy watches, and piling up more money. More important, I grew tired of seeing things happen that weren't in the best interests of clients and individual investors.

Since my "retirement" from Wall Street, I have earned my medical degree from UNC-Chapel Hill, done a research fellowship at Duke University, been published in a peer-reviewed scientific journal as a lead (or "first") author, and become a board-eligible ophthalmologist (eye surgeon).

I've also found the time to visit dozens of countries, pick up my pilot's license, and bottle my own vintage of cabernet sauvignon wine.

And while I loved studying medicine and helping people live healthier lives, I began to notice that the U.S. medical industry was corrupted by outdated thinking, corporate lobbyists, and ignorant government officials.

I knew I could help more people and live a richer life by writing about money and health. I knew if I could write about these topics – without the negative influence of lobbyists, bureaucrats, and corporate hacks – I could make a bigger difference to my "patients" and friends.

I say none of this to brag... only to show you that I've been fortunate enough to learn a lot over the years. I've met and worked with a lot of smart, successful people. I've worked with billionaires and future Treasury secretaries. I've encountered a lot of great ideas in my careers.

But without a doubt, one of the things I'm most proud of is leading the now-famous "demonstration" where thousands of investors learned how to harness an extremely powerful financial tool... and then use it to safely make millions of dollars.

All while taking little risk and sleeping well at night.

WHY I STARTED THIS CONTROVERSIAL DEMONSTRATION

In 2002 or 2003, while I was researching genetic eye diseases at Duke, I met a publisher named Porter Stansberry. After hearing about my careers in finance and medicine, he convinced me to write to his readers about my ideas.

We believed that together we could help people lead better lives if we could teach them some key concepts about health and wealth... concepts they likely wouldn't hear about from their stock broker or doctor.

The mainstream press is virtually forbidden from mentioning many of these concepts. Huge corporate interests and corrupt government institutions would rather people didn't know about them. The more ignorant people are, the better for many government and corporate interests. This keeps them dependent. It keeps the "nanny state" alive.

Well, in 2010, we began publishing a service called *Retirement Trader*.

The goal of the service was simple: To teach regular people how to use investment techniques that Wall Street banks and traders use to <u>safely</u> make millions – even billions – of dollars.

While some people think of these techniques as "advanced" or "complicated," they're actually very easy to learn. They are easy to use. And they can <u>drastically improve your investment results.</u>

Here's what subscriber J.C. told us:

"Thanks for translating options lingo into English for me. I have wanted to learn to trade options for some time but was intimidated by the special language used. I know it can be a great way to make money... Your simple and easy approach is great support for me as I attempt to embrace these strategies in my trading. Kudos to ya! More people deserve to have this opportunity."

I'm willing to say that the techniques we use in *Retirement Trader* form the greatest investment income strategy in the world. This strategy can be used to safely and conservatively generate 15% or more in annual income on a retirement account (or a regular portfolio).

I know this sounds like an outrageous claim. But judging by the feedback we've received from readers describing their "real money," those claims aren't "outrageous" enough.

From April 2010 to October 2013, we used this strategy to close 136 consecutive trading positions for a profit. We suffered no losses. And readers made millions of dollars.

Some folks used the strategy to earn annual income streams on their retirement accounts of more than 25%.

These big income streams were earned when interest rates were next to nothing... when the average investor could barely earn a few percentage points on their savings without taking huge risks.

The major reason we made so much money with such consistency is due to a wonderful "loophole" in human psychology.

As you'll learn in a moment, humans are hopelessly ignorant gamblers.

And that's a good thing.

> *I want to thank Dr. Eifrig for his patient and methodical approach to teaching this skill. He took all the fear away and managed to explain his system in plain English and with great accuracy. Kudos to Dr. Eifrig for making my retirement a much more financially secure adventure.*
>
> – Ozzie Z.

WHY THIS EXTRAORDINARY INCOME OPPORTUNITY EXISTS

Before we get into the specifics of safely making huge income streams, it's important to know why the opportunity exists...

It all comes down to gambling.

I know that sounds crazy. After all, I just said that you can earn 12%-20% annual yields on your money... <u>very safely.</u>

So you might be wondering how in the world "gambling" has anything to do with this approach.

Here's why...

A share of stock represents a slice of ownership of a company. As you probably know, these ownership stakes in thousands of businesses trade on stock exchanges.

You might have heard news stories that mention the price of Google stock... or ExxonMobil stock... or Apple stock. And it's likely that you've bought such a stock... or own some in your retirement account through various investment vehicles.

The stock market is full of gamblers... people who attempt to trade short-term price movements. They jump into and out of positions in a matter of days or weeks.

These gamblers don't pay much attention to the quality of the businesses they are buying. They're simply looking to make a quick buck on (often random) price movements.

These people treat the stock market as a giant casino... where they can gamble with thousands (even millions) of dollars for a shot of "hitting it big."

These gamblers love to trade "stock options."

Stock options are one of the most misunderstood financial vehicles. The mainstream press – and even your broker – will tell you options are inherently risky and virtually guaranteed to lead to financial ruin.

This is just not true. It's a crude and unsophisticated view of the markets. The real story is that when used properly, stock options can drastically lower your investment risk... while dramatically increasing your returns.

I know this statement probably goes against what you've heard about options. For most folks, it's like someone telling you that regularly eating burgers and fries is good for your health.

But in the case of stock options, what I've said is 100% true. Believing otherwise prevents people from making extraordinary returns... while taking little risk.

So let's repeat it again:

Counter to what most people believe, stock options can <u>drastically lower your investment risk... while drastically increasing your returns.</u>

The key is, we can use stock options to become "the house" that collects on bets that gamblers make on short-term market movements.

You see, the way most people use stock options increases the risk to their capital. But the strategy I'll show you uses stock options to decrease the risk to your capital.

Used in the conservative manner I'm about to explain, options can allow you to safely generate double-digit income streams in a retirement account.

We do it by collecting the money others gamble away.

TAKE HOME MESSAGE:

- Stock options can drastically lower your investment risk.

- I left finance and medicine to empower regular folk to use the same investment strategies Wall Street uses to make money.

- Some of my readers have increased their annual income streams to 25%.

HOW TO COLLECT MONEY LIKE A VEGAS CASINO

– 2 –

To start collecting safe, sleep-at-night income with this strategy, you need to understand some simple option concepts. We'll start with a basic definition.

A stock option is a contract between two parties that gives the buyer of the option the right – but not the obligation – to purchase or sell a security at a given price, during a given time period.

Stock options that allow you to buy a stock at a given price in the future are **call options.**

Options that allow you to sell a stock at a given price in the future are **put options.**

Don't worry if these definitions sound strange. Once we walk through a few examples together, "call options" and "put options" will be as understandable as buying insurance on your car... or maintaining a bank account.

THE EASY WAY TO UNDERSTAND OPTIONS

We'll get into how the "stock market casino" works in a moment. Before that, let's learn more about how options work.

Most people learn about options the best by thinking of them using a few housing examples.

Remember… there are two kinds of options – "call" options and "put" options.

Call options give the buyer of the option the right – but not the obligation – to buy an asset at an agreed-upon price at a given time in the future.

Put options give the buyer of the option the right – but not the obligation – to sell an asset at an agreed-upon price at a given time in the future.

We'll start with an example of how a call option would work if you could use one to trade your home.

Let's say you own a house with a current market value of $400,000.

One day, a gentleman knocks on your door. He believes good things are about to happen in the area around your house. Several big businesses are expected to move into town and create lots of new jobs. These new jobs will cause the price of local housing to increase.

This gentleman wants to profit from his expectation of a rise in the area's home prices. But he doesn't have enough money to buy a house.

So he tells you he'd like the right, but not the obligation, to buy your house from you for $440,000… six months from now.

He says he'll pay you $10,000 in cash immediately, if you agree to his terms... of letting him buy your $400,000 house for $440,000 six months down the road.

You start thinking...

You bought the house for $200,000 more than 10 years ago. You've been thinking about moving to a different state.

Plus, you've heard those rumors about businesses moving in before. They didn't pan out. You think the gentleman's expectation of your house being worth more than $400,000 in six months is fanciful. He's a bit of a gambler, in your opinion.

But... if this gambler is willing to hand you $10,000 cash in exchange for you agreeing to sell your home for a healthy profit, you'll gladly take his offer.

You say yes, and you both sign the contract. This contract, this "option" for the gambler to buy your house from you, is a "call option."

This agreement between you and the "house gambler" can have several different outcomes:

OUTCOME NO. 1:

Remember those businesses the "housing gambler" expected would bring jobs to the area? They arrive. They bring thousands of new jobs. Home prices rise substantially.

Your house appreciates in value by $60,000. It's now worth $460,000. According to your contract, you must sell your house to the gambler for $440,000. You keep the upfront $10,000 cash payment, sell your house for a profit, and find a new house.

The gambler put up $10,000 to purchase the right to buy

your house for $440,000, but he can turn around and sell it for $460,000. He makes a profit of $10,000. This doubles his original $10,000 stake. (We're keeping transaction costs out of this example to make it simple.)

OUTCOME NO. 2:

The businesses don't arrive. No new jobs are created. The value of your home remains $400,000 over the course of the six-month contract.

Remember, the house gambler purchased the right, but not the obligation, to buy your house from you for $440,000. Since the gambler has no interest in buying a house for $440,000 that is only worth $400,000, he walks away from the deal. You keep the $10,000 cash payment.

OUTCOME NO. 3:

One business arrives and brings some jobs to the area... but not enough to produce a substantial rise in home prices. The value of your home rises modestly... to $420,000.

Remember, the house gambler purchased the right, but not the obligation, to buy your house from you for $440,000. The gambler has no interest in buying a house for $440,000 that is only worth $420,000. So in this outcome, he walks away from the deal. You keep the $10,000 cash payment.

OUTCOME NO. 4:

The businesses don't arrive. No new jobs are created. One large local business actually leaves, which pulls jobs out of the area. The value of your home falls to $380,000 over the course of the six-month contract.

Again... the house gambler purchased the right, but not

the obligation, to buy your house from you for $440,000. He does not want to buy a house for $440,000 that is only worth $380,000. He walks away from the deal. You keep the $10,000 cash payment.

That's how a call option works. The buyer of the call option (the housing gambler) believed the price of your house would rise and wanted to profit from it.

The seller of the call option (you) was willing to sell the asset at the agreed-upon price. Call options got their name because the asset can be "called" away from the option seller.

Let's use another housing example to learn about "put options"...

Remember, an option is a contract between two parties. The acquirer of the put option – the buyer – is purchasing a contract that allows him to sell an asset at a given price in the future.

The seller of the put option contract is taking the other side of the trade. He is agreeing to buy an asset at a given price in the future.

I know at first this can sound complicated, so let's go over it one more time. The buyer of a put option gets the right, but not the obligation, to sell an asset at a given price in the future.

The seller of a put option agrees to buy an asset at a given price in the future.

Now... let's use another home-buying scenario. Say you're familiar with a particular neighborhood and the values of the homes in it.

You see an attractive little house that you think is worth $200,000. Paying $200,000 for it would be a good deal in your opinion.

But you're not interested in a "good" deal on that house. You're interested in a great deal.

You'd love to buy the house for $170,000... or 15% ($30,000) below the market price.

Here's where a put option contract comes in...

You approach the owner of the house and start talking. He's a nervous sort. You learn the homeowner – like most homeowners – is concerned about the economy, skyrocketing gas prices, the upcoming elections, and the world in general.

He's worried that something bad could happen to the country, which could cause the price of his home to sink to less than $150,000. He's even worried the house is only worth $180,000 to begin with.

You tell the homeowner: "Well, you never know what will happen in the world. But I think I can help you out. If you give me $2,000, I'll agree to buy your house for $170,000 if you want to get it off your hands. That offer is good any time for the next 12 months, no matter what happens."

The nervous homeowner agrees to your offer. You draw up a contract, you both sign it, and he gives you $2,000 cash.

This is generally how selling a put option works. You (the put option seller) enter into a contract with the homeowner (the put option buyer) that gives the buyer the right, but not the obligation, to sell that house to you for $170,000 sometime in the next 12 months.

The outcome can work out several different ways... (see sidebar).

OUTCOME NO. 1:

The "calamity" the homeowner is worried about does not arrive in the next 12 months, and home prices in the neighborhood remain robust. In that case, he won't be interested in selling his house for $170,000.

You keep the $2,000 and the transaction is finished... over... done.

OUTCOME NO. 2:

If the homeowner decides, for whatever reason, that he wants to sell you his house for $170,000 in the next 12 months, then you are on the hook to buy it for that amount... regardless of the current market price.

Remember, you believe it is worth $200,000. So you're thrilled with a $30,000 discount. And you keep the $2,000 you received upfront.

That's generally how put

OPTIONS ACT LIKE STOCK INSURANCE

When it comes to learning the basics of selling put options, many people benefit by viewing it like selling insurance...

When you insure your home, you are essentially buying the right to sell your house to the insurance company for a certain value, under certain conditions, for a limited period of time. In return, you pay the insurance company to accept those terms – whether or not you ever exercise the terms of the policy.

Put options work the same way. When you sell a put option, you're acting like the insurance company. You're agreeing to buy someone else's shares of a particular stock for a set price, under certain conditions, for a limited period of time.

In the case of your house, you'd exercise your policy in a disaster... when a fire or catastrophic weather damage wrecks the value of your home. In the case of a put option, the holder would exercise his right to sell us his stock if the market value of his shares falls below the price we agreed to pay.

One key to selling puts safely and profitably is KNOWING THE REAL RISKS IN OWNING A COMPANY'S SHARES. Just like the insurance company needs to know the details of your home (square footage, upgrades or renovations, what you paid for it, any valuables you keep there, etc.), we need to assure ourselves the companies we sell puts on are fundamentally sound.

We won't insure just any stock. We're going to identify stocks we like and would want to own. Then, we'll insure them at a price they are unlikely to fall below. No matter what happens, we win. If the stock falls, we buy a stock we wanted to own anyway at a better price. If the stock doesn't fall into our laps, we keep the insurance premium, free and clear.

options work. The buyer of a put option purchases a contract that allows him to <u>sell</u> an asset at a given price in the future.

The seller of the put option contract takes the other side of the trade. He agrees to <u>buy</u> an asset at a given price in the future.

HOW OUR HOUSING EXAMPLE WORKS IN THE STOCK MARKET

A few pages ago, we learned about "call options" by pretending we owned a house... and then sold someone the right to buy our house for an agreed-upon price at an agreed-upon time in the future.

Most people don't realize this, but these sorts of transactions happen every single day the stock market is open. But these transactions don't involve houses.

They involve stocks.

A share of stock represents the

ownership of a small slice of a business.

Some businesses chop their ownership structure into hundreds of millions of these "shares." These shares fluctuate in value every day the financial markets are open.

In addition to the big market for stocks, there is also a big market for stock options. Each day the market is open, millions of stock options are bought and sold. And a huge number of the participants in the stock-options market are hopeless gamblers.

We can use this market and its participants to produce steady income streams from the stocks we own in retirement accounts (and any other brokerage account).

Here's an example of how it works in the stock market...

Let's say you own 300 shares of stock in the hypothetical company Magnum Enterprises.

A few years ago, you bought the stock for $20 per share. Its current market value is $40 per share. Your holdings are worth $12,000.

One day, you look at the market and see that a group of stock market gamblers believe Magnum is about to experience a price rally. They believe shares could hit at least $44 per share within six months (a 10% gain).

They are willing to enter into contracts that give them the right, but not the obligation,

GAMBLERS OFTEN LOSE

Not every option buyer is a gambler in the way I've described.

Some people who buy options are conducting reasonable – and often sophisticated – financial plans. (I did plenty of this in my Wall Street career.)

But for our purposes, we don't need to focus on these participants. We're chiefly interested in collecting money from the gamblers.

to purchase shares of Magnum for $44 within six months. They will pay $1 per share for the right to enter into these contracts.

Just like our house example, these contracts, which allow people to buy an asset (in this case a stock) for a certain price at a certain time in the future, are named "call options."

The standard size of an options contract covers 100 shares. However, these contracts are quoted and priced in terms of just one share.

For example, if the quoted price of a call option contract is $4 per share, the call buyer would pay a total of $400 to acquire the contract.

If the quoted price of an options contract is $6, the call buyer would pay a total of $600 to acquire it.

One more time, for emphasis: **Option contracts cover 100-share blocks of stock. But they are quoted and priced in terms of just one share. A call buyer who buys a contract for the quoted price of $4 will actually pay a total of $400 for that contract.**

Options trade in bundles of 100 shares.

Option prices are in dollars per share.

Thus a $4 option price equates to $400 of option premium.

In the case of the stock market gamblers and Magnum Enterprises, the gamblers are paying $1 per share for the right, but not the obligation, to buy Magnum for $44 within six months.

If Magnum experiences a big rally, it could rise to $50 per share.

In this case, the gamblers win.

They can use their call option contract to buy Magnum shares for $44. They can then turn around and sell the same shares in the general market for $50 per share. They would make $5 for every $1 invested.

Why just a $5 profit and not a $6 profit?

Remember... in this case, the gambler paid $1 for the right to buy Magnum Enterprises for $44 per share. Thus, his "all in" cost in the stock purchase is $45 per share. When he sells his shares for $50, he makes a $5 profit, rather than a $6 profit.

Turning every $1 invested into $5 is an incredible gain in just six months. This type of gain would turn a $10,000 investment into $50,000.

It's this type of gain that attracts thousands and thousands of gamblers to the options market every day.

But just like big hits at a Las Vegas casino, big hits in the options market are extremely rare.

Most stock option gamblers lose their money... just like most casino gamblers lose their money in Las Vegas.

Still, the allure of "one big hit" draws huge amounts of people into the market... just like it draws them to Las Vegas.

No matter how many times people lose, they keep coming back. They keep gambling. It's just a quirk of human nature.

Thus, the vast majority of "call option" contracts that gamblers buy end up worthless. <u>The sellers of these contracts almost always keep the money the gamblers paid them.</u>

In Las Vegas, casinos occasionally have to pay out money to gamblers. But the odds are so stacked against the gamblers that casinos make billions of dollars a year.

The casinos make so much money that they can afford to build stupendous, lavish hotels. Their owners become millionaires and billionaires.

They make that money by taking the other side of foolish bets.

You can probably see where I'm going with this... and why my advice to investors is...

TAKE THE OTHER SIDE OF THE FOOLISH BETS... AND *SELL* CALL OPTIONS!

In our hypothetical case of Magnum Enterprises, the gamblers were willing to pay $1 per contract to bet on a price rise. They wanted the right to buy shares for $44.

Remember... a few years ago, you bought 300 shares of Magnum for $20 per share (a total cost of $6,000).

So you might be happy to sell your shares for $44. You would sell your holdings for $13,200 ($44 x 300). This is a profit of $7,200.

Because you'd be happy to sell your shares at a profit, you agree to sell your shares for $44 in six months. You sell the gamblers three call option contracts that cover your 300 shares.

The quoted price for this call option contract is $1. Since option contracts cover 100 shares of stock, but are quoted and priced in terms of just one share, you collect $300. (You own 300 shares... so you sell three contracts... each one netting you $100.)

Think about it this way... This $300 cash payment is a 5% "yield" on your original investment of $6,000.

Just as in our housing example, this deal can result in a variety of outcomes:

OUTCOME NO. 1:

Magnum Enterprises stages a big rally to $50 per share. The gamblers are right. They make big profits. Your shares are "called away" for $44 per share.

You keep the $300 cash payment and sell your shares for a profit of $7,200 ($13,200 minus $6,000).

OUTCOME NO. 2:

Magnum Enterprises moves higher... but only to $42 per share. Since nobody is interested in buying your shares for $44 when they can be purchased on the open market for $42, the contract is worthless.

You keep your shares. Plus, you still keep the $300 cash payment.

OUTCOME NO. 3:

Magnum Enterprises declines to $38 per share. Just as in Outcome No. 2, nobody is interested in buying your shares for $44 when they can be purchased for less on the open market. The contract is worthless.

You keep your shares. And of course, you keep the $300 cash payment.

I know this is a lot to take in, so let's review what happened:

- Just like in the housing example, you owned a valuable asset. In this case, it was 300 shares of Magnum Enterprises.

- You sold someone the right to buy your asset for an agreed-upon price at an agreed-upon time in the future. You collected a cash payment for entering this agreement. A gambler betting on a big price rise paid you the money.

That's it.

What you've done is known as "selling covered calls."

And it's one of the safest, easiest ways to generate large sums of cash on your savings.

> *I have invested my IRA funds into many of the stocks you recommended, and I have made 5.4% to date. I have tried a couple of your option plays and hope to continue to gain confidence in how to acquire more cash to re-invest!*
>
> – C. Erikson

A REAL-LIFE EXAMPLE OF SELLING COVERED CALLS... AND SOME NEW VOCABULARY WORDS

During the "demonstration" we talked about in Chapter 1 – when I closed 136 winners in a row – I showed readers how to constantly earn large cash payments with covered calls.

Let me walk you through a real-life example, so you can get a feel for how we do it...

In 2011, I showed readers how to sell a "covered call" on Microsoft.

I like investing in Microsoft because the ubiquitous software giant generates huge amounts of cash, enjoys a dominant position in its industry, and pays a steady and growing dividend.

In September 2011, Microsoft was trading for around

$25.90... which made it very cheap relative to its large earnings stream.

Because the company is so dominant and its shares were trading at such a cheap price, buying Microsoft was a very safe investment decision.

At the time, Microsoft's annual dividend payment was $0.64 per share... a dividend yield of 2.5%.

I encouraged my readers to buy Microsoft at $25.90... and then sell someone the right to buy their shares for $26 per share in November 2011. At the time, the contract for this deal was selling for $1.38

For every 100 shares they owned, readers received $138 for agreeing to sell their shares. (Remember, option contracts cover 100-share blocks of stock. But they are quoted and priced in terms of just one share.) With Microsoft trading for $25.90, buying 100 shares was a $2,590 outlay. The $138 payment resulted in an immediate cash yield of 5.3% on their investment.

In this example, the gambler would pay you upfront cash if you agree to sell him your Microsoft stake at $26 per share. (This $26 future price is called the **"strike price."**)

Selling your shares at $26 would reap a small profit (0.3%). But that $138 upfront payment (which is called a **"premium"**) amounts to a 5.3% yield on your original outlay of $2,590.

And remember... the agreement lasted until November 2011 (which we call the **"expiration month"** of the contract).

An investor at the time had to consider the two likely outcomes:

OUTCOME NO. 1:

Microsoft trades for more than $26 when the contract expires in November 2011. He would sell his shares for $26, a modest gain, and keep the $138 he received when he sold the call options.

Plus, he would get the quarterly dividend in November of around $0.16 per share, or another $16. Thus, he would make 6.3% in about two months.

OUTCOME NO. 2:

Microsoft does not trade up to $26 by November 2011. The gambler will not exercise his right to buy your shares since he can get them cheaper on the open market. So the contract expires worthless, and you keep the November dividend ($16) and the $138 he paid you upfront.

If you did this sort of "5%-plus in two months" trade six times a year, **you would collect more than a 30% annual income stream.**

In terms of cold cash, you would collect $828 a year in "premiums" on your initial outlay of $2,590... plus an additional $64 in annual dividends.

That's a 34.4% "yield" in 12 months on one of the world's safest stocks.

That's how my way of selling covered calls works. It's just two basic steps:

Step 1: You buy safe stocks.
Step 2: People pay you money for agreeing to sell your stocks for a profit.

It's that simple.

24

A great part is that unlike the housing example, you don't need someone to walk up to your door. You don't have to go out looking for these people. The options market is full of gamblers... and they are always willing to pay you money.

I know what you're probably thinking... *"Earn a safe 34.4% in just 12 months? It's not possible to earn that sort of yield in a safe stock."*

You're right for being skeptical. And for folks who don't use covered calls, it's virtually impossible to generate that much income on a stock. But believe me, when you learn the ins and outs of option selling, these sorts of returns are possible.

You won't always find opportunities like the Microsoft example I just showed you, but annual income streams of 12%-20% are realistic in a covered call account. And occasionally, you find exceptional opportunities like our Microsoft example.

Keep in mind, I didn't make that trade up out of thin air. I showed my readers of *Retirement Trader* that very trade in late 2011.

In our Microsoft example, we used a few terms that will likely be new to you. We used the term "strike price" and "premium." We talked about the "expiration month."

Because these are probably new terms to you, let's walk through them one more time. It's vitally important that you know these terms... just as it's vital that you know words like "turning signal" and "gear shift" to safely drive a car.

THE NUTS AND BOLTS OF SELLING COVERED CALLS

Let's return to our Microsoft example...

Remember, we bought <u>Microsoft</u> shares for $25.90 per share. We then sold someone the right, but not the obligation, to buy the shares for <u>$26</u> in <u>November</u>. We received <u>$138</u>.

The stock the option contract is based on – in this case Microsoft – is called the **"underlying."** The stock serves as the underlying base for the contract. The movements of the value of the contract are dependent on the movement of the underlying.

The payment we received – $138 in this case – for entering the contract is called the **"premium."** So a covered call seller might say "I received a premium of $138."

The "$26" figure is called the **"strike price."**

The strike price is the share price at which you will sell your shares at an agreed-upon time in the future.

Many different strike prices are available in the options market on any one underlying.

In the Microsoft example, contracts may exist with strike prices of $22, $23, $24, $25, $26, $27, $28, $29, and $30. An investor might not agree to sell his shares for $26... but he would sell shares for $27. In this case, the "strike price" in the option contract would be $27.

When you sell covered calls, you'll want to sell the option that has a strike price that is just a dollar or two above the purchase price of your shares.

In the 2011 Microsoft example, we agreed to sell our shares for $26 in November. November in this example is the **"expiration month."** The expiration month is the month that your contract expires.

Most option contracts last less than one year. And most stock options expire on the third Saturday of the month – Option Expiration Day.

Let's go over our transaction and the terms involved, one more time.

In our example, we bought <u>Microsoft</u> shares for $25.90. We sold the right, but not the obligation, to purchase our shares for <u>$26</u> in <u>November</u>. We received <u>$138</u> for agreeing to those terms.

Microsoft is the **underlying.**
$26 is the strike **price.**
$1.38 is the option **price.**
$138 is the **option premium we collect per option (equal to 100 shares).**
November is the **expiration month.**

We'll cover a few other concepts and terms later. But if you understand these four key concepts, **you're 95% on your way to being a successful covered call seller.**

You're on your way to <u>safely</u> earning 12%-20% annual yields on your savings.

To help you on your way, we need to cover another important idea when it comes to selling options for extra income.

Selling covered calls isn't the only aspect of a sound options strategy. It's a way to make extra cash on stock that you own. But there's a way to collect cash before you even buy the stock...

TAKE HOME MESSAGE:

- Don't use stock options to gamble in the market. Gamblers often lose.

- For every option traded, there's a buyer and a seller.

- Call options give the buyer of the option the right – but not the obligation – to buy an asset at an agreed-upon price at a given time in the future.

- Put options give the buyer of the option the right – but not the obligation – to sell an asset at an agreed-upon price at a given time in the future.

HOW TO GET PAID TO BUY STOCKS

– 3 –

Have you ever refused to pay full price for a car... a house... or a vacation?

If you're like me and know the first price you hear is always negotiable... you're going to make a great put option seller.

In Chapter 2, we covered a quick introduction to "put options."

Remember, an option is a contract between two parties. The acquirer of the put option – the buyer – purchases a contract that allows him to sell an asset at a given price in the future.

The seller of the put option contract takes the other side of the trade. He agrees to buy an asset at a given price in the future.

In our introductory explanation to put options, we used a simple housing example: You noticed an attractive house that you thought was worth $200,000. Paying $200,000 for it would be a good deal in your opinion.

But you were not interested in a "good" deal on that house.

You were interested in a <u>great deal</u>. You wanted a discount.

You wanted to buy the house for $170,000... or 15% ($30,000) less than the market price.

You approached the owner of the house, agreed to buy his house for $170,000, and received $1,000 for entering into the contract.

This is the core idea of selling put options. **You identify an asset you want to own... and agree to buy it at a discount to the market price.**

As I'm about to explain, it's a way to get paid on both sides of a stock purchase transaction.

<u>Selling puts pays you on the way in... while selling covered calls is a way to get paid on the way out.</u>

Since you've learned most of the key vocabulary words of stock option selling, we're going to jump right into a real-life example of how lucrative and safe selling put options can be.

A Real-Life Example

During my *Retirement Trader* demonstration, I showed readers how to turn semiconductor giant Intel into a money machine...

Technically, you'd describe Intel as a $100 billion computer-chip maker. But that description shortchanges how marvelous this business is.

Intel is a moneymaking machine. It is the dominant

manufacturer of the most essential component used in computers.

All of the name-brand computer makers – Microsoft, Dell, even Apple – rely on its processors. And electronics makers use its chips to improve the brainpower of everything from ovens to garage door openers.

To get a sense of how dominant Intel is, realize it controls about 80% of the global market for microprocessors. Its nearest competitor, AMD, accounts for just 10% of the market. Intel made $4.3 billion in net income in 2010. AMD, on the other hand, struggled to break even. It regularly loses hundreds of millions a quarter.

When 2012 rolled around, AMD was dying a slow death. Its cash flows were barely positive – only once in the previous three years. That meant more market share for Intel. Other competitors existed, but they couldn't match Intel for quality, price, or brand loyalty.

For all practical purposes, Intel has no competition. It's a virtual monopoly. With a profit margin of 23%, Intel has margins at the levels of some of the best businesses ever. And Intel treats investors who hold its stock well. In 2012, it paid shareholders an annual cash dividend of 4%.

Going back to our home analogy for a second, it's safe to say Intel is a beautiful, hurricane-proof, beachfront mansion. It's one of the world's ultimate blue-chip companies.

And yet, in 2012, the stock was trading for dirt-cheap prices.

In February 2012, Intel was trading for around $26.60 per share. For Intel shares, this price was a good deal. But remember... just as in the house analogy, I'm not interested in a "good deal" on Intel. I'll let the other guy settle for a "good" deal.

I want a great deal.

That's why I encouraged *Retirement Trader* readers to make a discount offer on Intel by selling put options.

At the time, we could sell a put option contract on Intel that obligated us to buy shares for $26 in April 2012. It was less than two months away.

This contract was priced at approximately $0.65 per share. And since one option contract represents 100 shares, we received $65 by selling this put.

Let's go over the math as if we were willing to buy 300 shares of Intel at the dirt-cheap price of $26 a share...

If we wanted to buy 300 shares of Intel, we would enter the market and sell three put contracts.

This would obligate us to buy Intel for $26 per share in April 2012. And as I mentioned, we'd receive $0.65 per share for taking on this obligation.

Since each contract represents 100 shares, we would receive $65 per contract. And remember, we want to buy 300 shares, so we will sell three contracts and receive $195.

What Happens After We Sell Put Options?

If we sell three put contracts that obligate us to buy Intel for $26 per share in April 2012, it can work out a handful of different ways...

OUTCOME NO. 1:

Intel stock chugs along... and advances from $26.60 per share to $28 per share. No Intel shareholder will sell us shares for $26 when they sell on the open market for $28. So, we simply pocket the $195 we received for selling the puts.

OUTCOME NO. 2:

Intel stock doesn't move at all. It remains at $26.60 per share on April 2012. No Intel shareholder will sell us shares for $26 when they can get more on the open market. So again, we pocket the $195 we received for selling the puts.

OUTCOME NO. 3:

Intel declines from $26.60 per share to $24. Plenty of Intel shareholders will sell us shares at $26 since that's $2 more than they're worth on the open market.

So we are "put" the stock. That means we are obligated to buy 300 shares of Intel at $26 per share... a $7,800 outlay.

Remember... we were paid $195 to enter into the put contracts. Therefore, our "real" cost was $7,605 for those 300 shares. That means our price was actually $25.35, not $26 per share.

This is the beauty of selling put options the *Retirement Trader* way. You spot a great company... and you decide the price at which you'd like to buy shares. By selling put options, you receive upfront cash, and you get to buy the shares at a discount to the current market price.

In our example, we agreed to pay $26 per share for Intel. This represented a 2.3% discount to the then-current price of $26.60 per share. And we were paid $65 for every 100-share block we agreed to purchase.

Here are the basics of our trade, with those vital option vocabulary words highlighted:

Intel is the **underlying.**
$26 is the strike **price.**
$0.65 is the option **price.**
$65 is the **premium (since contracts cover 100 shares).**

April is the **expiration month.**

We sold the April 2012 Intel $26 put options for $0.65 per share. Since contracts cover 100 shares but are priced per share, we received $65 per contract.

HOW TO PRODUCE HUGE INCOME STREAMS ON STOCKS YOU'VE BOUGHT

As you can see, selling put options lets you buy great companies at discount prices.

In Intel's case, the stock was already a good value at $26.60 per share. But we agreed to buy it at an even better price of $26 per share.

If Intel climbed in price (or stayed at $26.60 a share), we would not have been "put" the shares. We'd just keep our $65 premium free and clear.

If Intel declined below our strike price of $26, we would have been "put" the shares of the wonderful business that we wanted to own. And we'd keep our $65 premium.

In other words, selling puts is a way to get paid "on the way in" with your stock purchases. By selling puts on great companies trading for good prices, *Retirement Trader* readers were only "put" shares about 25% of the time during our first three years. But that 25% of the time, we ended up buying a great company at a discount price. We got paid to buy a valuable asset at a discount.

Once we were "put" shares of a stock, we would immediately start collecting dividends. We'd also begin collecting income by offering to sell our shares at higher prices...

We'd begin selling covered calls on the shares we owned.

As we covered in Chapter 2, when you sell covered calls, you collect upfront cash... and agree to sell your shares for a profit.

Let's go over that one more time: By selling puts, you collect cash <u>on the way in.</u> By selling covered calls, you collect cash <u>on the way out.</u>

Done properly, this strategy results in a constant flow of cash... all paid to you by the gamblers of the stock market. It's realistic to expect annual income streams of 12%-20% on a portfolio.

I know because I've done it personally for many years. And I've shown thousands of people how to do the same.

Let's walk through another real-life example of how you can make large, safe returns by pairing up a put and call selling strategy.

In July 2011, I encouraged *Retirement Trader* readers to sell the September $65 put on Johnson & Johnson for $0.95.

At the time of my recommendation, Johnson & Johnson (aka "J&J") shares were trading for around $66.60.

Selling this put option obligated us to buy J&J shares if they traded for less than $65 come that September. We were paid $95 for every contract sold. When you accounted for this premium, we would have been buying J&J for a real cost of $64.05 (strike price of $65 minus the $0.95 premium).

Most people are familiar with the J&J brand. Most people have purchased J&J Band-Aids before.

But what most people <u>don't realize</u> is that J&J is one of the best-managed companies of the past few generations. As of 2013, it boasts 50 consecutive years of increasing dividend payouts. (Keep in mind, most stocks can't even boast <u>five</u>

consecutive years of dividend payouts.)

In addition to Band-Aids, J&J sells other well-known products like Listerine, Imodium, Benadryl, Lactaid, Motrin, Nicorette, Pepcid AC, Rogaine, Tylenol, Rolaids, Neutrogena, Splenda, and Visine. It also rakes in billions of dollars every year by selling "blockbuster" prescription drugs and medical devices.

J&J regularly ranks at the top of "most respected" and "best managed" company lists. It's also one of a handful of elite companies with a pristine "triple A" credit rating. This prestigious rating is only given to companies with super-strong balance sheets. Boasting the triple-A rating is like saying your company is one of the biggest, strongest castles in the kingdom.

All these attributes lead market professionals to call J&J a "blue chip" stock. It's the best of the best. (Blue chips are traditionally the most valuable at the poker table.) It's the stock market equivalent of beachfront property.

But remember... in the stock market... even the share prices of elite blue-chip businesses can fluctuate. Shortly after my recommendation, the broad market experienced a big selloff. Plus, J&J was dealing with some minor short-term business setbacks.

When mid-September rolled around, J&J traded for $64.59 per share... or just a little less than our strike price of $65. Thus, the shares were "put" to us. We bought J&J stock at $65 per share. Remember though, by collecting the $0.95 premium at the start of the trade, our real cost was still less than our purchase price.

After we were "put" shares of J&J, we immediately got in line to collect J&J's safe and growing annual dividend yield of a little more than 3%. This added a second stream of cash flow into our account, in addition to the first stream, the put premium.

We added a third stream of income to our account by selling covered calls against our shares. Remember, by selling covered calls, we collect upfront cash for agreeing to sell our shares at a higher price than we paid for them.

In this case, we sold the November $65 calls for $1.60. This premium represented an instant payout of 2.5% on our real cost of $64.05. It also obligated us to sell our J&J shares for $65 come November.

When November came around, J&J shares were trading for less than our strike price of $65. Our shares were not "called away." We took this opportunity to sell another round of calls. We sold the January 2012 $65 calls for $1.22 a share. This represented an instant payout of 1.9% on our real cost of $64.05. Another stream of cash.

While waiting for mid-January 2012 to roll around, we collected J&J's quarterly dividend payment of $0.57. When mid-January 2012 arrived, J&J was trading for more than our strike price of $65 a share. Our shares were "called away" for a profit.

I'm a 45-year-old stay-at-home mother with very young children ages nine and four. This is the BEST income strategy I have ever encountered. I'm up nearly $9,000 in a little over 5 1/2 weeks.

– Brenda E.

COUNTING UP THE CASH... WE COLLECT THREE DIFFERENT INCOME STREAMS

This particular example demonstrates how investors can collect cash three different ways by selling options on dividend-paying blue-chip stocks.

We collected cash by selling the put. We collected cash from J&J's dividend payment. And we collected cash by selling covered calls.

By themselves, these individual income streams are not huge. But when you add them all up, the returns are fantastic, considering we are holding such a low-risk stock.

Here's how the numbers stack up:

In July 2011, we sold the September 2011 $65 puts for $0.95.

After being put the stock, we sold the November 2011 $65 calls for $1.60.

In November 2011, we sold an additional round of calls for $1.22.

In November 2011, we collected the $0.57 quarterly dividend.

In January 2011, we sold our shares for $65.

Here's how the math looks:

```
    $0.95 for the September $65 puts
 +  $1.60 for the November $65 calls
 +  $1.22 for the January $65 calls
 +  $0.57 dividend
    ─────────────────────────────────
 =  $4.34 total cash received per share.
```

Over the seven-month life span of the trade, we collected an income stream of $4.34 a share on a $65 stock (a 6.7% yield). This is an annualized gain of around 11.4%.

And remember, we collected this income by holding one of the world's strongest, safest stocks.

In the first three years of *Retirement Trader*, we were "put" shares only 25% of the time. But when we were put, we started collecting dividends and covered call income.

This "income from all directions" strategy allowed us to close 136 consecutive positions at a profit... and allowed readers to collect annual income streams of 12%-20% on their stocks.

Yes... These trades happen all the time.

I know you might think this sounds too good to be true, or that I'm "cherry picking" some rare example.

That couldn't be further from reality...

We began publishing *Retirement Trader* in July 2010. Over the next three plus years, we closed out 136 trades in a row that revolved around this concept of selling puts.

If you are worried that all of this sounds too complicated for you to do, don't worry. I promise you, it's pretty simple once you've done a few of these trades on your own.

I'm so sure people can easily make these trades, I offer a 90-day trial period to my subscribers.

Over the years, I've taught a lot of people how to do this – everyone from accountants and chemists to car dealers, construction workers, and U.S. military personnel. One fellow, a mechanical engineer for the energy industry recently told me he's made $60,000 trading this way – just in the past 10 months. *Heck, I've even taught the worst investors in the world – doctors – how to do this!*

39

Doctors are notoriously bad at investing. I know this from my time in medical school and residency. They think that they know it all... But I've taught a dozen or so doctors how to do this successfully.

Here's what one doctor, R.G., told us:

"I am a vascular surgeon and appreciate your good investment and medical advice and education. Keep up the good work and thanks again."

TAKE HOME MESSAGE:

- Selling put options allows you to buy great companies at a discount.

- You can realistically make 12%-20% a year using this strategy.

- Anyone can do this, even the worst investors in the world.

WHY YOU SHOULD OWN THE BEST... AND STICK WITH BLUE CHIPS

– 4 –

Many folks hold a common misconception about selling options.

These people have tried an unsophisticated, risky approach to selling options. So they have come to believe ALL option selling is risky.

These people miss a key component of safe option selling. Once again, we can explain this component by talking about real estate...

Blue-chip stocks are the stock market's equivalent of beachfront property.

Beachfront property is always in demand. It resists down markets better than undesirable locations. It's the best.

You see, the premiums an investor can collect by selling options on risky, volatile stocks are typically higher than the premiums he can collect on safe, steady blue chip stocks, like Microsoft or Coca-Cola.

Stock options are more expensive on volatile stocks than they are on safer blue chips.

So, tempted by the allure of larger cash premiums, many investors sell options on risky stocks. And yes, these investors might collect a big cash premium, but they put themselves in great danger by taking on the potential obligation of buying and owning risky stocks.

When selling puts, you're obligated to buy the stock. So be sure you'd want it.

With risky option selling, an investor might buy a "hot" technology stock for $40 per share, and then sell someone a call option that will let him buy the stock for $45 in six months.

Let's say the covered call seller receives $3 per option in premium (since option contracts cover 100 shares but are priced per share, the seller receives $300).

Now imagine the risky tech stock acts just like a risky stock often does... and falls by $15 per share. Even though the covered call seller received $3 in premium, he has suddenly lost $15 per share. Of course, he's only down $12 because he took in $3 of option premium.

Owning risky stocks is a big risk in conventional investing. And it's also a big risk in covered call selling.

That's why I want you to stick with the best, strongest, safest stocks in the world. I want you to stick with blue chips. Blue chips typically have extremely robust business models... wide profit margins... big competitive advantages... and low debt levels.

> *I'm holding stocks in my accounts like Intel, Cisco, Exelon Energy, which I've been assigned and feel good about making money on these positions as the months go by. I don't miss trying to trade stocks like Green Mountain Coffee, Netflix, and other volatile stocks that keep me up at night. I look forward to refining my trading techniques and taking this trading platform into my retirement in the next few years.*
>
> – T.W.

The stock we studied in Chapter 3, Johnson & Johnson, is a great example of a blue chip.

If you're unfamiliar with the term, know that "blue chip" is the label given to world-class businesses that dominate their industries.

These attributes make blue chips the safest stocks in the world... and perfect for conservative investors.

I'm sure you've used the products and services of many blue-chip businesses...

You've probably enjoyed a soda made by Coca-Cola, one of the best companies in the world. You've probably used a computer with software by Microsoft. You've probably covered a cut with a Band-Aid made by Johnson & Johnson. You've probably had a burger at McDonald's. You've probably fueled your car at a gas station owned by ExxonMobil.

These are the kinds of stocks that you should own in your retirement account. These stocks almost always feature one of the keys to a great retirement stock: **They pay steady and growing dividends.** And I love dividends because...

'DIVIDENDS DON'T LIE'

A dividend is a distribution of company's earnings. It's a way for the owners of a company to collect an immediate return on their investment. And remember... when you own shares of stock, you hold a small ownership stake in that company.

Dividends are often quoted in terms of the "yield" they offer investors.

For example, if a stock has a share price of $10 and pays a $0.50 per share annual dividend, the "dividend yield" is 5%.

Smart, sophisticated investors have a saying about these payments made to shareholders: *"Dividends don't lie."*

Here's what I'm talking about: A good accountant can fudge 99% of the figures on a balance sheet or a profit statement. But he can't fake a cash payment.

For example, take Wall Street's favorite number – earnings. Earnings are subject to all sorts of bookkeeping adjustments like depreciation, reserve accounting, and different inventory valuations. Because investors pay attention to earnings more than any other number, it becomes really tempting to manipulate them.

But think about a dividend. A dividend is a fact. When companies pay their dividends, they mail out checks to every shareholder.

If a company is paying cash, it's hard to fake the numbers. The money leaves the bank and never comes back. It's that simple.

Regular dividend payments are a real mark of quality. The management and directors know their company better than anyone else. So when a company announces a dividend

44

payout, it's saying, "We have cash we don't need."

A strong dividend payment almost always indicates a healthy business. The company is generating cash and wants to say "thank you" to shareholders.

And a company knows if it takes the dividend away suddenly, its stock will drop. It's not always easy to pay out cash to the shareholders every year...

Cash is a scarce resource, and it's critical to every business. So when companies are able to maintain their dividends through bad times, it sends a strong signal to the market that management knows what it's doing... that it has good control of its company's finances.

Similarly, rising dividends protect stock prices in bear markets. Thus, dividend stocks are by nature "defensive stocks." They protect your capital. A rising dividend acts like a pontoon float and prevents the stock price from falling much.

Finally, a dividend payment signals management's intention to reward investors for offering their capital. As a stock analyst, I place great weight on the dividend payments when I size up a company. A regular and increasing dividend payment is a sign of a healthy business.

For example, Coke is one of my favorite stocks. It has paid a dividend for 50 straight years. Or take one of my favorite drug-maker stocks, Eli Lilly. It has paid a dividend for 43 straight years.

These types of blue-chip companies carry much less price risk than the typical risky stock carries. They rarely fall 15% in a hurry, like the "hot" tech stock I discussed in our example.

However, blue-chip stocks aren't exciting enough for

most people. Most people would rather gamble on risky technology stocks, or on something "exciting" like the initial public offering of Internet social-media service Facebook.

When it comes to selling options the *Retirement Trader* way... and generating safe income on your nest egg... we want big, safe, companies that plow relentlessly forward like a bulldozer. Those are the investments that allow us to sleep at night while owning them.

Listen to what subscriber A. M. told us about investing in blue chips...

> *I'm 63, own my own business, still working, & love Retirement Trader. I have made about $30,000 using Doc's tips. The list is long: Exelon, Microsoft, Medtronic, Intel, CVS, and more. I like it so much, I have taken back my professionally managed IRAs and intend to do them myself, using Doc's tips.*
>
> *I have been an investor for 30-plus years. You name it, I have invested in it. Some good, some not so good. What I find most attractive about Doc's approach, is the relative low risk. If a put doesn't work out, I end up owning a great company, (hurt me again). It's literally the best approach I have ever seen, then used, then made money, consistently...*
>
> – A.M.

We may not be able to predict which tech company will produce the next hot gadget. But it's a sure bet that tomorrow, people will still drink Coke, still buy burgers at McDonald's, and still use Johnson & Johnson's Band-Aids. They'll be doing all this 10 years from now.

By sticking with blue chips in our covered call strategies, we don't mind if our shares decline a little. We still collect premiums. We still collect dividends.

By sticking with blue chips with our put-selling strategies, we win either way. If the stock rises in price, we simply keep the premium. If the stock declines in price and we are "put" the stock, we don't mind. We end up buying a quality business at a price we think is a bargain. We can then start collecting dividends and covered call premiums.

Once again: Avoid the risky method of selling options...

Stick with the best! Stick with beachfront real estate! Stick with blue chips!

[In Appendix I, you'll find a list of my favorite blue-chip companies.]

TAKE HOME MESSAGE:

- Avoid gambling on risky, "exciting" stocks.

- Focusing on blue-chip stocks lowers our risk of selling option.

- A common characteristic of great companies is a long history of growing dividend payments.

HOW TO 'UNLOCK' YOUR BROKERAGE ACCOUNT AND GET STARTED

– 5 –

Just like you fill out forms for a doctor's visit or a bank account, you'll need to fill out forms to get started as an options seller.

But as you're about to learn, it's all much simpler than anyone thinks.

First, let's talk about money and how much you'll need to get started.

I recommend people have at least $15,000 in savings to start selling options. Once you have that amount of money, you'll need to set up your account for both *margin* and *option* approval.

The government requires all options be held in what is called a "margin account."

That might sound intimidating, but don't worry: My mother has her own margin account.

To kick off this process, you simply need to ask your broker for "margin approval to sell (put and call) options."

You should know upfront that some brokers and advisors might tell you that you can't or shouldn't be doing this. That's because many people use options to increase the risk in their account.

Remember, a lot of hopeless gamblers are out there. Brokerages often put up a little resistance so they can say, "I told you so" (even though they badly want the business).

Once the margin approval is in place, you'll also need to authorize your brokerage account for trading options. (Realistically, you'll do both of these at the same time.)

Your broker can provide you with what is called a "standardized options agreement."

In the standardized options agreement, you'll need to ask for approval for both covered options as well as naked put selling (or "writing," as it's called). "Naked" simply refers to selling options without simultaneously owning shares of the underlying. It's the opposite of "covered."

In most cases, you can get the forms online, fill them out, and either fax them back or mail them to your broker. Your account should be approved shortly thereafter.

And if by chance your broker doesn't think you're capable of handling options, fire him on the spot.

I prefer Fidelity and TD Ameritrade... But most of the top-10 names in the business can open options accounts for you easily and quickly.

Going through these steps and seeing new terms might be new to you. But don't let it frighten or worry you.

Remember... most people think of INCREASED risk with

margin accounts and options. On the other hand, we are using margin accounts and options to REDUCE risk.

When you request broker approval to trade options, the broker will assign you a "level" of authorization, typically Level One to Five. The levels relate to your trading experience and the varying degrees of risk carried by different options trades.

For our put strategy, most brokers will require you to have "Level Three" or up to "Level Five" option approval. The exact levels can vary from broker to broker. But don't worry if they claim your experience doesn't warrant you Level Four approval.

In each issue of *Retirement Trader*, we modify the trades to accommodate all levels of option approval... We call these trades, "IRA Alternatives." An IRA Alternative is a covered call. And these trades are almost identical to the put trades we recommend. You can perform covered call trades with even the lowest level of options approval.

The main difference is that they won't let you do the naked puts in the lower levels... but the return difference with interest rates so low is meaningless.

Once you've opened the account, you'll need to learn how to enter orders. Your online broker's trading platform should offer you the choice to "sell to open" a "put" or "covered call" trade within a drawdown box or click button.

If you're unsure, call the brokerage's customer service desk and have someone walk you through the screens... Just don't ask them to do the trade for you. It can be prohibitively expensive to transact with a live person.

I prefer to use discount brokers. You interact mainly with the company's website. These brokers normally don't talk with you on the phone unless absolutely necessary (and they charge more if you transact with them over the phone).

In exchange for accepting less human contact and spoon-feeding, discount brokers charge much lower your transaction fees – which means more money for you.

You should know that I don't have *any* financial relationship with *any* of broker. Although I like TD and Fidelity, I've heard great things about Interactive Brokers and TradeKing.

TAKE HOME MESSAGE:

- Everyone needs to open a brokerage account.

- You can start with just $15,000.

- When setting up your brokerage account, make sure you get both margin and option approval.

- Good discount brokers – like TD Ameritrade, Fidelity, and Charles Schwab – let you open options account quickly and easily.

THE EASIEST OPTION APPROVAL LEVEL: COVERED CALLS

− 6 −

OK... we've covered the basics of option selling. We've learned to base our option selling around blue-chip stocks. And we've got our options accounts up and running.

Now... let's get down to specifics. Let's learn how to enter our orders.

We'll cover how to enter a "covered call" order first.

As we cover this information, remember that each online broker is a bit different... but the mechanics of entering a covered call position are relatively uniform across the brokerage world.

It involves a few simple steps that are always the same:

STEP 1: TRADE

After you log into your online broker, you'll need to access the "trading platform" inside your brokerage account.

The trading platform is the individual webpage where you can input the specific details for each trade.

The trading platform will usually be listed under a "Trade" or "Trading" tab on the webpage.

STEP 2: OPTIONS

Once you're inside the trading platform, you'll notice various types of securities available for trading (for example, stocks, bonds, mutual funds, etc.).

Find the tab that says "options" and click on it.

If your broker has only given you approval for the most basic option trading level (Level 1), you will be able to execute covered call trades.

If you've been authorized for a higher level, you may see more types of trades open to you (for example, "spreads," "butterflies," or "condors"). Ignore these odd sounding terms. But no matter your level, the type of trade you want to do is called a "buy-write" – or covered call – trade. Look for that term and click on it.

STEP 3: BUY-WRITE (AKA COVERED CALLS)

Remember, "buy-write" and "covered call" refer to the same type of trade. When making a covered call trade, you are performing a two-part transaction. You are "buying" the shares and "writing" the call contract (i.e., selling calls) in tandem. That's why it's also called a "buy-write" trade.

For the first part, you'll input the information on the stock you wish to buy.

Remember, you'll want to purchase shares in increments

HOW STEVE BURNS IS CHARTING A WHOLE NEW RETIREMENT

Steve Burns is a practicing ophthalmologist living in Las Vegas, Nevada.

In addition to helping patients with their vision for 18 years, Steve has always been fascinated by finance and investing. He graduated with a minor in finance and started investing more than 15 years ago. From stocks, bonds, options, futures, and real estate... Steve tried just about everything to make steady income. And he did pretty well for himself especially in real estate...

"Over the years, I have learned to enjoy the steady income from real estate bringing a consistent 12% return," Steve told us. *"The frustration has been with my retirement accounts invested in the market."*

Then in 2008, the market collapsed. Steve – like many individuals – saw his retirement portfolio suffer. Steve moved most of his money into gold. He realized he needed to a way to generate steady, safe income from his stock investments, no matter what

of 100, since each option contract you sell covers 100 shares of stock. So, if you plan on writing one call contract, you will first need to buy 100 shares of stock.

STEP 4: TWO PARTS TO THE TRADE – SHARES AND OPTIONS

After you've input all the information for the shares you wish to purchase, the first half – the "buy" component – of the buy-write trade is complete. Now you just need to enter the options details to complete the second half – the "write" portion – of the covered call trade.

You'll input all the details found in an options trade: the order type (in this case, "sell"), the number of contracts (for 100 shares, select "1" contract), the type of option (in this case, "call"), the expiration date, and the strike price.

You'll then select price, price type, and term. (I'll

the economy or the market was doing.

Before subscribing, Steve said his option trading experience was "unsuccessful." But now, Steve says his returns have been fantastic. *"I've made 40% this year already,"* using the education he received from Dr. Eifrig...

"My frustration ended with the knowledge [Doc has] shared with the ability to generated steady income from stock ownership," Steve said. *"I don't feel I am speculating when I buy a stock now, but owning a company and just 'renting' my shares."*

After just a year and a half, Steve is looking forward to retirement. He's even started flying lessons. In 2012, he wrote in to say:

"Thank you! Thank you! I see a whole new retirement ahead for me now."

come back to these terms in a moment.)

STEP 5: ALWAYS PREVIEW THE TRADE

Once you've entered all the information for both stock and option, your trading platform might display a "preview order" page that will present the total cost of this two-part transaction.

The price comes from the stock price while subtracting the option premium for the call option, to give you what's called a "net debit." It's a debit because you're paying them money directly from your account.

For example, let's imagine a buy-write on a stock that is trading for $39 a share with call options going for $1. That means your net debit is $38 ($39 minus $1).

STEP 6: EXECUTE THE TRADE

Once you've reviewed the information for accuracy, click "execute trade" to make the trade "live."

I know this may seem a little confusing at first. But trust

me, it's much easier than you may think.

If you'd like a more detailed description of what to expect when entering a trade online, please check out our supplementary report "The Retirement Guide to Buying Securities." Call the Stansberry & Associates customer service team at 888-261-2693 to receive a free copy. When you call, we'll also give you a risk-free trial to my newsletter, *Retirement Millionaire*, along with the free report.

Beyond our report, your brokerage website has a "help" section to explain what the various terms mean. Plus you can still call or chat with your broker online to clear up any questions or concerns you may have. (Just don't trade through a live person as it's more expensive.)

TAKE HOME MESSAGE:

- There are six simple steps to selling covered calls.

THE 'MORE ADVANCED' OPTION APPROVAL LEVEL: UNCOVERED PUTS

– 7 –

In the last chapter, we learned how to enter "buy-write" covered call orders. As you've discovered by now, it's much easier than it may seem.

Now, let's learn how to enter an uncovered (or "naked") put order.

The funny thing about selling naked puts... The process requires even fewer steps than selling covered calls. Still, brokerage houses consider these trades "more advanced" than selling calls because we may make the transactions on margin. (We'll explain margin in a minute.)

Regardless, the mechanics of the trades couldn't be simpler.

Each online broker is a bit different... but the process of entering a naked put position is relatively uniform across the brokerage world.

It involves a few simple steps that are always the same:

STEP 1: TRADE

After you log into your online broker, you'll need to access the "trading platform" inside your brokerage account. Just as we explained with covered calls in Chapter 6, the trading platform is the individual webpage where you can input the specific details for each trade.

The trading platform will usually be listed under a "Trade" or "Trading" tab on the webpage.

STEP 2: OPTIONS

Once you're inside the trading platform, you'll notice various types of securities available for trading (for example, stocks, bonds, mutual funds, etc.).

Find the tab that says "options" and click on it.

Since you've been authorized to trade at a higher level (typically around Level 3), you may see more types of trades available. These may include things like "spreads," "butterflies," or "condors." Ignore these odd sounding terms. The type of trade you want to do is a basic, uncovered put trade.

STEP 3: UNCOVERED PUTS
(AKA NAKED PUTS)

Selling uncovered puts is simpler than selling covered calls. It's a one-step transaction. There's no need to buy a stock first, before selling the option.

To begin the actual trade, you'll first need to input the underlying stock's ticker symbol. This will usually bring up extra data, like the current price and trading volume of the stock.

Next, you'll input all the details found in an options trade: the order type (in this case, "sell"), the number of contracts (for 100 shares, select "1" contract), the type of option (in this case, "put"), the expiration date, and the strike price.

You'll then select price, price type, and term. (I'll come back to these terms in a moment.)

STEP 4: ALWAYS
PREVIEW THE TRADE

Once you've entered all the information for the stock option, your trading platform should display a "preview order" page that will present the total cost of this transaction.

The dollar amount shown comes from the number of contracts you've agreed to sell, and the amount of premium you will receive for each. The buyer of the put contract(s) pays you to agree

Selling puts requires something that selling calls does not... a surplus of ready cash.

You need to have funds available to purchase shares if you are put the stock on options expiration day. The amount of surplus funds required to sell put options depends on the type of account you have.

- If you are conducting this trade within an IRA account, you will need to have enough cash to cover the full cost of the shares (even if you never get put the stock).

- If you are using a regular brokerage account to conduct the trade, your broker will only require you to keep a portion of the total stock purchase price in cash. This "margin requirement" acts like a security deposit for the broker. It reassures him you can meet your obligations if you're put the stock. The margin requirement may vary by brokerage... but it is typically 20% of the full purchase price.

Remember, each put contract you sell covers 100 shares of stock. If you are put the stock, you will be required to buy 100 shares of stock at the agreed upon strike price.

to purchase the stock at the strike price you agree to.

For example, let's imagine a put contract on a stock that is trading for $39 a share. At the moment, these put options are going for $1. If you sell one contract, you will receive a premium of $100 ($1 x 100 shares per contract).

Remember, you will be required to purchase the full amount of stock if the stock price falls below the strike price on options expiration day. If this happens, selling one put contract requires you to buy 100 shares of stock for $3,900.

STEP 5: EXECUTE THE TRADE

Once you've reviewed the information for accuracy, click on "execute trade" to make the trade "live."

This may seem a little confusing at first, but it's much easier than you may think.

If you'd like a more detailed description of what to expect when entering a trade online, please check out our supplementary report "The Retirement Guide to Buying Securities." Call the Stansberry & Associates customer service team at 888-261-2693 to receive a free copy. When you call, we'll also give you a risk-free trial to my newsletter, *Retirement Millionaire*, along with the free report.

Beyond our report, your brokerage website has a "help" section to explain what the various terms mean. Plus you can still call or chat with your broker online, to clear up any questions or concerns you may have. (Just don't trade through a live person as it's more expensive.)

TAKE HOME MESSAGE:

- There are five simple steps to selling uncovered (or "naked") puts.

OPTIONS FIT INTO A SAFE, SENSIBLE LONG-TERM WEALTH PLAN

– 8 –

The single most important factor in your investing success has nothing to do with selling options... or picking the right stocks.

It has nothing to do with paying attention to what the president or Congress say.

It has nothing to do with the state of the economy.

It has nothing to do with knowing how to "time the market."

The single most important factor in your investing success is 100 times more important than any of those things.

Ignorance and mismanagement of this factor ruin more retirements than every other factor combined. Yet, most investors never give this idea any thought...

So far we've discussed how trading covered calls and naked puts works. And we've walked through the steps for opening an options-trading account and how to execute a trade. But before we launch into building a portfolio of options positions, you must understand some critical investing concepts and how our options fit into a balanced portfolio...

The first vitally important idea is called "Asset Allocation."

I hope I have your interest... because once again, I've found that ignorance of this idea destroys more retirements than any other financial factor.

But if you understand the ideas in this chapter, there's no reason you can't use this idea to create a lifetime of safe wealth generation.

WHY FINANCIAL INSTITUTIONS WON'T EVER TALK ABOUT THIS WITH YOU

You'll almost never hear folks in the finance and investing industry mention the words "asset allocation."

You won't hear it from brokers, who spend their days pitching stock ideas to their clients. Nor will most of my peers in the publishing industry mention it. And forget about a discussion of the topic on the cable news providers, like CNBC.

The reason is, asset allocation is simply boring. It doesn't sell.

People would much rather buy research about a hot pick than read about asset allocation. Since the customer is paying the bills, that's what he gets.

But if you're not quite familiar with what asset allocation means, don't be intimidated... it's easy to understand.

Simply put: Asset allocation is how you balance your wealth among stocks, bonds, cash, real estate, commodities, and gold.

This mix is the most important factor in your retirement investing success.

Keeping your wealth stored in a diversified mix of investable assets is the key to avoiding catastrophic losses. It's the key to keeping your retirement as safe as possible.

If you keep too much wealth – like 90% of it – in one or two stocks and the stock market goes south, you'll suffer badly no matter how good the companies are.

Or if you quit your nursing job to move to Florida and put all your wealth in rental real estate, you'll be wiped out in a big real estate crash (like many folks were in 2008).

The same goes for all asset classes... gold, oil, bonds, real estate, blue-chip stocks, etc.

Concentrating your retirement nest egg in just a few stocks or a few different asset classes is way too risky. *Keeping your eggs in one basket is always a fool's game.*

And although selling options on blue-chip stocks is an incredible way to collect income, even this strategy needs to fit inside a larger, diversified wealth plan.

I always encourage my readers to avoid placing their hard-earned money on one number and spinning the roulette wheel. We prefer to play the odds and keep them in our favor... something that produces plenty of safety and upside. Here's how you should think about asset allocation...

THE FOUR ASSET CATEGORIES
YOU ALWAYS NEED

The idea of allocating assets across different categories is based on the mathematical phenomenon known as "correlation." Without going too deep, correlation – specifically *positive* correlation – means that when one asset goes up in price, the other does, too.

Looking back in history, we can measure the correlations (or lack of correlation) among many asset categories. And we know that assets like cash, stocks, bonds, and gold are correlated to different factors. That means holding some of each at all times will protect you from catastrophe in one of the asset categories.

You need to understand four key asset classes...

CASH IS KING (10%-45%)

Our first category to consider is cash...

"Cash" simply means all the money you have in savings, checking accounts, certificates of deposits (CDs), and U.S. Treasury bills. Any investment with one year to maturity or less can be considered cash.

And here's an amazing fact... Over the past 36 years, holding cash in your portfolio has returned more than either stocks or bonds 17% of the time.

Of course, over the past century, stocks have averaged around 9%, bonds 7%, and cash only 4%. Still, it is important to know that in one out of every six years, cash is king.

I like to remind myself to increase the amount of cash in the later days of bull markets when stocks are expensive. This lets me raise cash to use when stocks are cheap again.

Legendary investors flush with cash are able to get assets on the cheap after prices move to more normal valuations. They swoop in and pick things up with cash quickly, often at great prices.

One of the major tenets of good financial planning is to always have six to 12 months of living expenses in cash in case of personal or job disaster. Before investing in anything else... start building your cash stash until you have at least three months available.

I generally recommend holding between 10%-45% of your assets in cash, depending on your circumstances.

ALWAYS OWN STOCKS (25%-70%)

If you want to get wealthy over time, the best way to do it is through our second allocation category – stocks.

Over long periods of time (say, seven to 10 years), stocks outperform all other types of investments. And since timing the market is not easy to do, we always want to own stocks along the way.

Most people already know this, but few understand how it happens. It doesn't happen slowly, it happens very quickly.

Researchers with the brokerage Fidelity found that $10,000 invested in the Standard & Poor's 500 in 1980 grew to $300,000 by 2007. *But if you missed just the best 30 of those 7,000 days, you would have made only $51,000.* Miss the best five days, and you only make $90,000. Think about that... *If you missed the five best days over a 27-year period, your return drops from 2,900% to 800%.*

It's hard to imagine anyone picking exactly which five days

to be invested in stocks. That's why you should always own stocks. No other passive investment vehicle compares with stocks.

Whether you're just beginning to invest or a 40-year veteran of the markets, the one question you should always ask is, "What percent of my portfolio should be in stocks?"

The answer depends on several factors...

First, how old are you... and how much risk do you want to take?

One guide to determine what percentage of your portfolio you should dedicate to stocks is the "100-minus-age" rule.

Just take 100% and subtract your age. So if you're 60, the rule says you should have around 40% of your portfolio in the stock market. But if you're a bigger risk-taker and have plenty of income or assets to live on in case the market takes a prolonged nosedive (as it did in Japan for 30 years), you might consider increasing that another 10% or 20%.

However, if you're 75 years old, 25% may still be a little high for you. And that brings us to our third question...

How are the valuations of the stocks determined in the stock market?

Legendary investors – guys like billionaire Warren Buffett and Peter Lynch who built Fidelity Investment's Magellan fund from $18 million in assets in 1977 to $14 billion by 1990 – were always looking for low-priced companies that produce great products and services. But to buy at great prices, you have to look at the metrics of the market.

By this, I mean metrics like price-to-earnings (P/E), price-to-book-value (P/BV), dividend yield, and debt-to-balance-sheet ratios. Many long-term studies show that investing when stock metrics are high bring worse results than investing in the same stocks when the metrics are low. So if we're above a P/E ratio of 16, P/BV of 3-4, or dividend yields below 2%, owning less stock is usually the prudent thing to do... especially if stocks have been performing well relative to other assets.

I recommend holding anywhere between 25% and 70% of your portfolio in stocks.

THE CORNERSTONE OF INVESTING: FIXED INCOME (10%-50%)

Fixed-income securities are designed to pay a regular stream of income over a fixed period of time. At the end, you also get most of your initial investment (called principal) back, depending on what price you paid at the start.

Depending on your age and tolerance for risk, bonds sit somewhere between boring and a godsend. The promise of interest payments and an almost certain return of capital at a certain fixed rate for a long period of time lets me sleep well at night.

Including safe fixed-income securities to your portfolio is a simple way to stabilize and balance your investment returns over time, too. For people with enough capital, locking up extra cash (after you've saved six to 12 months of your expenses) in fixed-income is a great way to generate much more cash flow than the nearly nonpaying money-market or savings accounts.

One beauty of bond-holding comes from a concept called "seniority."

This means if a company gets into financial trouble,

bondholders get their money before others. (Stockholders are last in line.) This fact alone makes it easier to own bonds than stocks – especially if you're more than 70 years old (the age when most folks need to be overwhelmingly concerned with preserving their retirement money and income... not so much concerned with increasing their net worth).

Adding safe fixed-income investments into your portfolio is a simple way of stabilizing your investment returns and guaranteeing wealth without worry. Knowing you will get a check from the government or a company before anyone else is a great feeling.

One of the things I like to do with a bond allocation is invest in bond-focused mutual funds. With these investments, we're pooling our money with other investors and minimizing the risk from any one or two bad investments. Since the fund holds dozens of individual bonds, we're instantly diversified. If one bond defaults, we've got the safety of the others to hold our value and income relatively constant.

In general... I recommend holding anywhere between 10% and 50% of your portfolio in fixed-income assets, depending on your needs for income and your worries about owning stocks.

CHAOS HEDGES (1%-15%)

Our fourth broad category of assets to have in a portfolio is what I loosely call "chaos hedges."

As the U.S. government continues to spend more than it takes in... and attempts to improve business conditions by increasing "money printing," there's always the chance that we'll see a collapse of fiat money worldwide.

But I don't think it's likely that the reserve currency, the dollar, will be the first to go. It's more likely the euro or the yen collapses before the dollar. So holding a small percent of your assets in what I call "chaos hedges" is like having an insurance policy.

Hard assets like gold, silver, timber, and even farmland historically provide comfort and protection during rough political and economic times. That's why we've just seen the large rotation of investment funds into gold and farmland, even after a decade-long run up in gold and silver prices.

The problem is, the value of these more commodity-like assets can change quickly. Take the collapse of gold in 1980 when it fell 40% in just two months. That's why I urge people to hold only a small portion of their assets in these sorts of hedges.

When interest rates are negative – when inflation is higher than interest on short-term fixed-income securities – that's the ideal time to own precious metals and land and timber.

Until only recently, gold had negative returns for several decades. In fact, it's still well below the inflation-adjusted price of $2,200 it reached back in January 1980. Yet, if you believe like I do that precious metals have their place in both times of geopolitical tension and economic stability, then a small position in chaos hedges greatly enhances your portfolio returns – as we've seen the past several years.

USING ASSET ALLOCATION TO STAY CONSERVATIVE

There's no way anyone can provide a "one size fits all" asset allocation plan to a large group of people.

Everyone's financial situation is different. Asset allocation advice that will work for one person can be worthless for another.

But most of us have the same basic goals: Wealth preservation... picking up safe income... and safely growing our nest egg. We can all use some guidelines to help make the right individual choices.

If you're having a hard time finding great bargains in stocks and bonds, I think an allocation of 25%... even 50% in cash is a good idea.

This sounds crazy to some people, but if you can't find great investment bargains, there's nothing wrong with sitting in cash, earning a little interest, and being patient. If great bargains present themselves, like they did in early 2009, you can lower your cash balance and plow it into stocks and bonds.

As for stocks, if you're younger and more comfortable with the volatility involved in stocks, you can keep a stock exposure to somewhere around 33%-50% of your portfolio. A young person can grow very wealthy by placing a sizable chunk of money into a group of high-quality, dividend-paying stocks and holding them for decades.

If you're older and can't stand risk or volatility, consider keeping a huge chunk of your wealth in cash and bonds... like a 75%-85% weighting. Near the end of your career as an investor, you're more concerned with preserving wealth than growing it, so you want to be very conservative.

When it comes to determining YOUR asset allocation mix, the big thing to keep in mind is that you've got to find a mix that is right for you... that suits your risk tolerance... your station in life. Whatever mix you choose, just make sure you're not overexposed to an unforeseen crash in one particular asset. This will ensure a long and profitable investment career.

Spend an hour or so each year thinking about your situation and goals. But in the interest of preserving your nest egg, err on the conservative side.

TAKE HOME MESSAGE:

- The most important factor in your investing success is asset allocation.

- Asset allocation is how you balance your wealth among stocks, bonds, cash, real estate, commodities, and gold.

- At a minimum, you need to allocate your money among cash, stocks, fixed income, and chaos hedges.

HOW TO LIMIT YOUR LOSSES

– 9 –

Once you've started trading and appropriately allocated your portfolio, the next step you need to take is to protect your portfolio from losses.

The best way to limit losses is to use a "stop loss" order. A stop is the downward limit you set for a security. Simply put, a stop loss is a predetermined price at which you will sell shares, regardless of anything else happening with the company or in the market.

There are two types of stop losses – a simple stop loss and a trailing stop loss. A simple stop does not move, even if your investment moves upward. Here's an example... Say you buy a stock for $10 and set a simple stop of 25%. This means you'll sell the stock if the price falls 25% from $10 to $7.50. Even if the stock climbs to $20, your stop will remain at $7.50.

A trailing stop loss adjusts higher as the share price of our investment rises. This locks in profits. (I mostly use trailing stops in *Retirement Trader*.)

For example, if you buy a stock for $10 and set a 25% trailing stop, you would sell the stock when the price falls 25% lower than $10 (down to $7.50). So far this is the same as a simple stop loss...

But if the stock rises to $20, your new trailing stop would be $15 (25% lower than $20). Setting $15 as the absolute floor for this position locks in a 50% gain on the position.

Is there anything magical about 25%? No. You can use any percentage. Sometimes we'll set our stops at 50% for more volatile recommendations and 15%-20% when we want to play conservatively.

With trailing stops, the discipline is what matters most. Sell when you hit the trailing stop, no matter what. Following this strategy will improve your investment returns immediately and dramatically.

Using a strict rule to avoid capital losses when we're wrong removes the emotions from the trade. When we're wrong, admitting it and taking our lumps is the most important part of trading successfully.

Good investors know: Losses are part of the game, and small losses don't matter.

Poor investors see every loss as a failure. But small losses aren't failures. They are victories – victories against big losses. You must avoid big losses at all costs. Nobody can survive a big loss.

Always define your losses when you initiate the position. I usually limit my capital losses to no more than 1% of my portfolio on any one trade. I do this by:

- Keeping my position size 4%-5% of the portfolio, and
- Limiting my loss with protective stop loss orders of 20%-25% on those positions.

POSITION SIZE	STOP LOSS	POSSIBLE LOSS
4%	20%	0.8%
4%	25%	1%
5%	20%	1%

Thus, 4% times 25% or 5% times 20% equals only a 1% loss in my portfolio. If we make 2%-3% on the winners (of similarly small size) in 60% of our portfolio, we'll do fine. Your winners should more than make up for your losers – as long as you keep your losses small.

WHAT ABOUT CALCULATING STOPS WITH OPTIONS?

Figuring out your stop loss for options isn't as hard as you might think. But the math is slightly different for calls and puts.

When you're selling a call, you use the entire amount of capital you need to execute the trade to calculate your stop loss.

Let's use one of the real trades we made in *Retirement Trader* as an example...

In November 2010, we sold calls on computer networking giant **Cisco (Nasdaq: CSCO)**. Here's the trade:

Buy 100 shares of Cisco (Nasdaq: CSCO) for about $21, and sell, to open, a CSCO December $21 call option for $0.68 or more.

77

That represented a total outlay (or "net debit") of $20.32 ($21 stock price minus $0.68 we received in call premium).

Remember... we bought 100 shares for every call option sold against the stock. Here's how the math worked:

Income from sold call premium of $0.68 is $68.00
Purchase of 100 shares of CSCO at $21 is $2,100.00

Initial outlay: $2,032.00

That initial outlay represented the cost of the trade.

Three things could have happened over the next month with this trade...

- Shares traded for less than $21 and the option expired worthless. In this case, we would have kept our shares of CSCO and the $68 in premium income.

- Shares traded for more than $21 and our shares were called away. In this case, we would be obligated to sell our CSCO shares at $21 a share, which we would have added to our $68 in premium.

- We hit our stop loss.

To figure out the stop limit, just take the combined value of the position and multiply it by 75%.

In the case, the combined value was $2,032 (cost of the shares minus the premium income)... $2,032 multiplied by 75% is $1,524. If shares of CSCO fell to $15.24, we would have sold the shares.

Of course, you'll have to simultaneously "close" out our call option position too, but it would likely be worthless at that point.

You would lose 25% on the position. But since you should

be using no more than 4% of your portfolio for this trade, you would lose no more than 1% of your trading capital.

To determine stops for puts you have sold, look at how much you'd value the underlying stock. For example, say you sell one put option for $1 with a $21 strike price. Recall each option contract represents 100 shares. So if the put were exercised and you were required to buy 100 shares of stock, you'd owe $2,100. Subtract the $100 you received in premium upfront, and your "capital at risk" equals $2,000.

So, you would set your stop at around $1,500 ($2,000 x 75%, using a 25% stop). If shares traded down to $15, you'd buy back the put to close out the position. (At that point, the options would be trading for around $6.)

When selling puts, don't worry about percentage changes in the market value of the puts... again, focus on changes in you capital at risk. Here's how that works...

If you sell one put option for $1 with a $21 strike price, your maximum capital at risk is $2,000 (recall each option contract represents 100 shares).

If you set a 25% loss, the most you want to lose on you capital at risk is $500 ($2,000 x 25% = $500). So to calculate the stop for the put option price take $500 and divide that by 100 shares. This makes your maximum loss $5 per option.

Since we opened the position by selling the puts, we would close the position by buying back those puts. And remember, when you first sold the put, you received $1 per option. That's your money to keep, and it raises your stop...

To ensure you incur a net loss of no more than $5 per option, you would buy back the puts if the option price increases to $6.

Here's the math:

$500 maximum capital-at-risk loss
÷ 100 shares (per option sold)
_____

$5 loss on the option price

If you hit your stop, you have to close your position. Here's the math...

-$6 the price of the option bought back to close position
+$1 income from selling the put option
_____

-$5 (This is the loss per option, which is $500 per contract)

Now if you're trading on margin, that $500 is going to feel like a lot more than 25%. But remember, when calculating your risk by trading options, the amount you pay upfront is far less important that your potential obligation. That's why we talk about capital at risk... how much money you would owe if the option were exercised against you.

Since the amount of capital you were risking is $2,000 (the $21 strike 100 shares per option), the stop loss is meant to prevent a loss of more than 25%, or $500, in the capital at risk.

HOW TO INCLUDE DIVIDENDS
IN YOUR STOP LOSS

When you're buying shares of stock or even selling a call option, it's important to factor dividends into your trailing stop loss.

That's because dividend payments change the point at which you would have to close your position.

Let me show you an example (when you're just holding shares of stock)...

If you're buying a stock for $10 and setting a 25% trailing stop, you would sell the stock when the price falls 25% lower than $10 (down to $7.50). If the price moves to $20, your new stop would be $15.

Let's say you received a $1 dividend payment. All you need to do is subtract that $1 dividend from the highest share price $20 in this case. Then, you use that number – $19 ($20 minus $1) – to set your stop loss. So your stop would move from $15 to $14.25 ($19 times 75%).

As you can see, dividends give you a little more downside protection.

The same is true with stops on options. And factoring dividends into your stop losses on options positions is just as simple. Let's take a look at an example...

You've bought a stock for $10 a share and sold a call option for $1. Recall, a call option controls 100 shares of stock. So this means your initial outlay is $900 ($1,000 for the 100 shares you purchased and $100 in premium for the call option you sold).

If the stock didn't pay a dividend, you would set your stop at $675 (your initial outlay of $900 multiplied by 75%). But let's say the stock pays you a $0.50 per share dividend ($50 per 100 shares). This would lower the cost of your position to $850 – the initial outlay of $900 minus $50. To calculate your stop you just multiply this new cost ($850) by 75%. This would give you a new stop of $637.50.

HOW TO MONITOR
AND TRACK STOP LOSSES

Tracking your stop losses does not require you sit by your computer all day. You have several options for tracking stop losses. Before we get into how to track your stops, let me just tell you the one thing you should never do.

Never enter your stops in the market!

ALWAYS keep your trailing stop-loss levels private and never share them with your broker.

Why? Entering your stop with your broker allows other traders to see where your stop is set. If the market nears that point and lots of investors have set stops at about the same price, the professional, high-volume traders (called "market makers") can move the market to trigger those stops, knowing once the selling is done, the price will quickly rebound.

Let me repeat...

Never enter your stops in the market!

Yahoo Finance is one of the simplest and cheapest (it's free) ways to track stops. It offers a simple service to track your stops and create alerts for them. If you don't already have a Yahoo account, it's easy and free to sign up. (But it's currently only available in the U.S.)

You can also use Tradestops.com, a service founded by a longtime Stansberry & Associates subscriber named Richard Smith. Richard initially built his website to follow *True Wealth* editor Steve Sjuggerud's trailing stop loss recommendations. Since then, he's turned it into a place where anyone can monitor his individual stops. It'll send you an e-mail alert when the market hits your trailing stop loss.

Richard's service is much more flexible than Yahoo's. Among other things, it allows users to set many different parameters for your stops, including volume, dates, and moving averages. It costs about $80 per year. (Please note, my publisher Stansberry & Associates recently became a partner in Richard's business.)

If you're interested call 1-866-385-2076 and ask about our current TradeStops deal. If you give them the code "Doctor," they can give you my current half-off deal for subscribers.

Several brokers now offer e-mail alerts. You can enter prices in their systems, which alert you via e-mail as well. Personally, I use Yahoo because I watch news, sports, and health information from my Yahoo homepage. But do what feels best and easiest for you.

TAKE HOME MESSAGE:

- Use stop losses to protect your portfolio from big losses.

- Never enter your stops in the market.

FIVE COMMON REASONS INVESTORS AVOID OPTIONS

– 10 –

No book on selling options would be complete without mentioning some objections people have to the idea.

Here are some common objections I've heard from readers and that I've found on the Internet:

REASON NO. 1: Option selling strategies like covered calls are too risky. You'll earn 5% in premiums, but if the stock falls 25%, you're still down big!

DOC EIFRIG ANSWER: This objection is 100% valid. As I mentioned earlier, the way most people approach covered calls is risky. They buy risky stocks because risky, volatile stocks typically offer larger cash premiums than safe, stable blue chips, like Intel. But most people end up losing on risky covered-call positions because the stocks falls in value.

A risky mining stock or fad retailer can fall 20% in one

day. That's why we avoid them. It's too much risk in our retirement account. You can mitigate this risk by <u>only buying and selling covered calls on the world's safest blue-chip companies.</u>

But by sticking with dominant, stable stocks like Coke, Intel, and Johnson & Johnson, the covered-call seller enjoys a tremendous layer of safety. These stocks generate big cash flows, pay steady dividends, have strong balance sheets, and great brands. You'd be happy to own these stocks for many, many years.

Reaching for extra premium in risky, volatile names is a loser's game. Leave the risky names for the "gamblers."

REASON NO. 2: Selling options is too costly. It generates too many brokerage fees.

DOC EIFRIG ANSWER: Selling options does generate more brokerage commissions than conventional stock ownership. But if you stick to the system I've described, and sell covered calls about six times a year on any given position, it's not a big problem.

For example, if you have a $25,000 portfolio, you might perform 20-30 covered call transactions per year. This many transactions would cost about $200 to $300 with an average low-cost online broker. The income generated by an intelligent covered-call program more than makes up for the increased brokerage fees.

If you have a tiny portfolio (like $1,000-$2,000) excessive brokerage fees are a danger. Your account is also too small to buy 100 shares of most blue-chip stocks. If you have a small amount of capital, you'll need to accumulate more capital in order to make selling covered calls a viable plan for you.

REASON NO. 3: Selling options is too much work.

DOC EIFRIG ANSWER: I always laugh at this one. Why?

Because most good things in life require work!

Investing is like anything else... If you're willing to learn and put in a little extra work, you'll be far more successful than people who are ignorant and lazy.

If you're not willing to learn something new and do just a little bit more work to generate much higher returns, then investing your money on your own is probably not for you. You're better off giving your money to a broker or mutual fund manager.

So to the objectors out there, yes, selling options is a little more work than conventional stock investing. But I've found that to achieve great results in any walk of life, you have to do some work (often a great deal of it). To get a high-paying job, you have to learn a useful skill. To start a great business, you have to learn how to provide customers with useful services or products. In order to achieve better results in anything, you have to learn... and you have to do extra work.

This work – of selling a few options each quarter and monitoring your portfolio will take about 30 minutes a month. I think it is well worth spending that extra time to generate safe, double-digit yields on a nest egg.

REASON NO. 4: Selling covered calls is too hard to understand.

DOC EIFRIG ANSWER: I know the world of stocks and stock options can be intimidating. But I learned this stuff just out of high school years ago. The finer points I learned at Goldman and on Wall Street. If I could learn it at 17, anyone can learn it.

But as I detailed in the housing example at the start of this course, by selling a covered call, you are doing two simple things:

1. You are buying a valuable asset, in this case a stock.

2. You are selling someone the right, but not the obligation, to buy that asset from you at a higher price than your purchase price. You collect instant cash for doing this.

That's it.

Don't worry if the smaller details sound confusing at first. Learning how to do most things requires some work... and multiple reads of how-to-guides. I encourage you to read this book several times...

Once you get the hang of things, selling options is as easy as managing a checkbook. The only math involved is on the fourth-grade level.

REASON NO. 5: I can't trade options in my IRA.

DOC EIFRIG ANSWER: This is not true. You can sell covered calls in an IRA. You just need to contact your broker and tell him you want to be approved for selling covered calls in your IRA.

It's natural when starting something new to feel nervous and a little unsure of what you're doing... I urge you to push through those feelings. Subscriber K.C., a registered nurse, did. And here's what she told us...

"I just started option trading last Jan (2012) and it wasn't until May (2012) that I had enough nerve to sell any puts... and

wouldn't you just know it, I sold 3 puts last May and ALL 3 got "put" to me. But I did NOT panic, I sold covered calls on all 3 of them at least twice and 2 of the stocks eventually got "called" and I made over $10,000 in capital gains! I totally understand that Doc's trades are STILL WINNERS even when you end up buying the stock... you're just not done making money yet. I feel much more confident making trades that Doc suggests over my own!"

HOW TO MANAGE YOUR PORTFOLIO OF BLUE-CHIP COVERED CALL POSITIONS

Once you know the "nuts and bolts" of building a covered call position... and once you know to stick with blue-chip stocks, you're ready to think about managing a full portfolio of these stocks.

For example, an investor has to think about some key concepts in order to safely manage his portfolio over the years. We'll treat them as a "Question & Answer" session.

QUESTION: How many covered call positions should be in my covered call portfolio to ensure it is adequately diversified?

DOC EIFRIG ANSWER: Five is good; 10 is better. But your total account size will affect decisions here.

Since you need to buy 100 shares to sell one covered call contract, a 100-share position on a $20 stock would be an investment of $2,000. A 100 share position on a $16 stock would be an investment of $1,600. A 100 share position on a $55 stock would be an investment of $5,500.

For example, if you have a $15,000 account, you'll be able to buy five stocks that have shares priced at an average of

$30 per share. In mid-2012, one could buy 100 shares each of blue chips Walgreens, Cisco, Intel, Exelon, and Wells Fargo for less than $15,000.

This portfolio would give you a good portfolio of consumer goods (Walgreens), network equipment (Cisco), semiconductors (Intel), utilities (Exelon), and banking (Wells Fargo).

I'd like to see investors own 10 stocks for better diversification, however. Since a good amount of the world's best blue chips trade for share prices in between $50 – $75, portfolios of at least $30,000 are required to diversify your portfolio beyond five stocks. But a $15,000 portfolio with four to five stocks is a good way to get started.

If you can, try to evenly spread your portfolio into five to 15 different positions.

QUESTION: When should I add a new covered call position?

DOC EIFRIG ANSWER: When you have enough cash in your account to buy a great company at a great price.

While I've provided the names of my favorite blue chips, market conditions change by the week. You want to ensure that not only are you buying the world's best business, but you are also buying them at good prices. This ensures you get good value for your investment dollar.

I recommend getting a subscription to an advisory or newsletter that tracks great blue-chip dividend-paying companies, and advises readers when to buy them.

I enjoy *Stansberry's Investment Advisory*, written by my friend Porter Stansberry. I also recommend following along with my own monthly advisory, *Retirement Millionaire*.

Each of these services does a good job of monitoring high quality businesses, and advising their readers when great values appear.

QUESTION: Is there ever a time I should consider selling out of one of my blue-chip stocks?

DOC EIFRIG ANSWER: Only if there has been a serious impairment to the business. Much of the time, a sell off in a blue chip is due to one-time, inconsequential issues... like a product recall or a court fine.

Remember... companies like Coke, Intel, and Johnson & Johnson dominate their industries. They've held their industry positions and rewarded shareholders for decades. It's very unlikely that something serious will come along and cause a material impairment to their businesses. That's the beauty of owning stable blue-chips. We get to safely compound our wealth for many years.

That said, anything can happen in this world... so it's important to check in on your stocks once every month or two. As I mentioned, a good advisory service can be a big help in this department.

THE TOP 25 STOCKS TO SELL OPTIONS ON

– APPENDIX I –

I've mentioned many times, option sellers should focus on blue-chip stocks in order to make the safest, steadiest gains.

Basing an option-selling strategy around risky stocks is a recipe for disaster. Remember, our goal is safe, consistent, income generation, not rapid capital gains.

The best way to achieve this goal is by loading our portfolio with shares of blue chips.

As I mentioned earlier, blue chips are the best, most stable businesses in the world. They share common traits like consistent profit margins, top name brands, thick profit margins, global reaches, cash-rich balance sheets, and steady dividend payments.

I know many people are too busy to dig through balance sheets and perform financial analysis, so I've provided a list of 25 excellent blue-chip stocks I encourage my readers to focus on.

25 EXCELLENT BLUE-CHIP STOCKS

No. 1:   GlaxoSmithKline (NYSE: GSK)

No. 2:   Exelon (NSYE: EXC)

No. 3:   Microsoft (Nasdaq: MSFT)

No. 4:   Eli Lilly & Co. (NYSE: LLY)

No. 5:   Cisco (Nasdaq: CSCO)

No. 6:   Medtronic (NYSE: MDT)

No. 7:   CVS Caremark (NYSE: CVS)

No. 8:   Abbott Laboratories (NYSE: ABT)

No. 9:   Johnson & Johnson (NYSE: JNJ)

No. 10:   Walgreens (NYSE: WAG)

No. 11:   United Technologies Corp. (NYSE: UTX)

No. 12:   Wells Fargo (NYSE: WFC)

No. 13:   Oracle Corp. (Nasdaq: ORCL)

No. 14:   Coca-Cola (NYSE: KO)

No. 15:   3M Co. (NYSE: MMM)

No. 16:   McDonald's (NYSE: MCD)

No. 17:   ExxonMobil (NYSE: XOM)

No. 18:   V.F. Corp. (NYSE: VFC)

No. 19:   Automatic Data Processing (Nasdaq: ADP)

No. 20:   Chevron (NYSE: CVX)

No. 21:   Colgate-Palmolive (NYSE: CL)

No. 22:   Target Corp. (NYSE: TGT)

No. 23:   Hormel Foods (NYSE: HRL)

No. 24:   The Clorox Company (NYSE: CLX)

No. 25:   The Walt Disney Company (NYSE: DIS)

Take a moment to identify and learn why these companies are some of the best in the world. They will become your portfolio's best friends... and your route to consistent income streams.

Please keep in mind... this list was compiled in early 2013. And while the basic characteristics of these businesses won't change much over time, some of the numbers are specific to early 2013.

For our current Top 25, visit the *Retirement Trader* website at *http://www.stansberryresearch.com/products/Retirement-Trader*.

NO. 1: GLAXOSMITHKLINE (NYSE: GSK)

GlaxoSmithKline (NYSE: GSK) started as a London pharmacy in 1715. It went global in 1830, opening its first U.S. pharmacy in Philadelphia. Today, GSK is a more than $100 billion global health care company with sales in more than 190 countries and one of the world's leading pharmaceutical companies.

GSK diversifies its business risk by selling many different types of drugs – not just a handful of blockbusters. It has a profitable stable of consumer product brands... from Aquafresh toothpaste to Beano (antigas aid) to Zantac (antacid medication).

Besides the biotechnology and drug interests, GSK takes the steady cash flows from its consumer product and drug lines and does two marvelous things with them: 1) It pays shareholders a big, steady dividend... and 2) It uses them to fund an innovative drug pipeline business.

One of the things I like to see in any large company is management returning excess profit to shareholders as opposed to stuffing their paychecks. GSK does this perfectly. The officers' pay is reasonable and less than most other businesses. GSK gives excess money back to shareholders through buybacks and dividends. This is the sort of respect for shareholders I like to see from every company we invest in.

NO. 2: EXELON (NSYE: EXC)

Exelon Corporation (NYSE: EXC) operates the largest fleet of nuclear-fueled power plants in the U.S. and the third-largest in the world. Exelon provides power to more than 6 million homes in Illinois, Maryland, and Pennsylvania, and nuclear energy accounts for more than 92% of that electricity.

EXC is the most efficient power generator in the nuclear energy business. Its 17 nuclear reactors have run with the fewest days offline (known as "down days") among all U.S. nuclear producers. This means EXC doesn't need to supplement its power production with other more expensive sources of fuel as much as its competitors do.

Further, its bottom line doesn't get hit when gas and oil prices rise. That makes EXC more profitable. Other energy companies that rely on gas or coal must seek higher rates from local governments to cover rising costs. Nuclear-power generators can easily get the same rate increases – but without the corresponding increase in fuel costs.

The nuclear companies keep chugging along with even higher operating margins... which means more money for investors. When coal and gas prices popped to record highs in 2008, EXC kept making money. When those fuel costs plummeted a year later, EXC kept making money.

NO. 3: MICROSOFT (NASDAQ: MSFT)

Computing software giant **Microsoft (Nasdaq: MSFT)** operates around the world in many segments of the computing business and gaming world. Everyone uses (or at least knows about) Microsoft's software or computing systems. In 2013, the company sold almost $78 billion in goods and services. It sold almost $74 billion the year before... Microsoft knows how to make money.

MSFT does a couple things we like to see in a good business. First, it generates tons of cash. MSFT produced $62 billion from 2011-2013. Second, the company is paying some of that extra cash back to shareholders. It distributes a bond-like 3.1% cash dividend and regularly buys back outstanding shares.

MSFT pays out billions in dividend to shareholders and regularly buys back shares. With fewer shares outstanding, our percentage ownership keeps rising. For a computer technology company, this sort of return to shareholders is unheard-of.

NO. 4: ELI LILLY & CO. (NYSE: LLY)

Eli Lilly & Co. (NYSE: LLY) is one of the world's best-known family names in the drug business...

Founded in 1876 by Civil War Colonel Eli Lilly, it's now the 10th-largest pharmaceutical company in the world. With a long history of drug discovery and market leadership, it is best known for its discovery of insulin. Other drugs and cures for anemia and hospital infections sit on a long list of successes.

Today, the company presents a great income opportunity.

Lilly is virtually unrivaled in its commitment to paying

shareholders. It has paid an annual dividend since 1885. The dividend streak puts it in the top 35 companies in the world for managing its money.

Perhaps more impressive, only one in 11 major drug companies (out of 348 total firms in the sector) pays a dividend at all.

Overall, Lilly is one of the perfect retirement stocks... low price-to-earnings (P/E) ratios, safe dividends yielding more than corporate bonds, and a consistent corporate strategy of rewarding shareholders.

NO. 5: CISCO (NASDAQ: CSCO)

Cisco (Nasdaq: CSCO) makes the routers and switches that enable information to move through the Internet and airwaves. Its products are everywhere. You can find its equipment in businesses, hotels, and homes. Hilton hotels use Cisco equipment. Starbucks uses Cisco to provide wireless Internet access. The phone on my office desk and the router in my home are Cisco-made.

One of the great things about buying mature technology businesses like CSCO is that they maintain large market share and can continue growing through acquisitions and developing new products. For clients to switch from one brand to another smaller brand gets harder and more expensive over time.

CSCO shows steady growth across business segments and geographic regions. Router growth was up 11% year-over-year. Some people are fearful that Cisco's growth is peaking. But given the company's growing dominance in its industry and rising dividend, this looks like a company poised to grow as the volume of information flow for the Internet grows.

In 2011, Cisco started paying a dividend of $0.06 per share and buys back billions of dollars of shares annually.

NO. 6: MEDTRONIC (NYSE: MDT)

Medtronic (NYSE: MDT) has been synonymous with pacemakers for years. But it's much more than that. In 1949, Earl Bakken and his brother-in-law Palmer Hermundslie founded a simple electronics-repair business in their Minneapolis garage. More than 60 years later, the company has ballooned into a $16 billion global leader in the medical-device industry.

For generations, Medtronics has been a leader in using electronics to stabilize and manage heart rhythms and maintain lives. It was one of the first to create an implantable pacemaker that could withstand the giant magnets of an MRI machine.

But the company has grown and diversified. In 2010, the Cardiac Rhythm division represented only 33% of the company's total revenue ($15.8 billion).

Today, Medtronic gets about 20% of its revenues from cardiovascular devices (e.g., heart valves). It derives another 20% from spinal products; it's a leader in scoliosis management. The rest comes from its neuromodulation – regulating the nervous system – (10%), diabetes (8%), and surgical technologies.

Medtronic remains a solid, well-managed company. In perhaps the toughest economic times, MDT grew revenues more than 9% from 2009-2011.

But the most exciting thing about Medtronic is how it

rewards its shareholders. The company has paid a dividend since 1977. Imagine a cutting-edge medical technology company that keeps growing and paying its investors.

MDT has positioned itself in life-sustaining technologies and is spreading into quality-of-life technologies. It's creating things like neuromodulation devices to stimulate the brain out of depression or Parkinson's disease. And it's working on diabetes implants that act like the real organs...

NO. 7: CVS CAREMARK (NYSE: CVS)

If you're a one-stop shop for health care, you should make good money the next 15 years, as the aging Baby Boom generation demands more health care. That's why I'm bullish on the future of one of the best drugstore chains in the U.S. – **CVS Caremark (NYSE: CVS).**

CVS operates mainly in the U.S. with three segments: Retail Pharmacy (7,327 CVS drugstores in the U.S.); Pharmacy Services (47 retail specialty pharmacy and mail-order businesses); MinuteClinic (657 retail health clinic outlets).

CVS Caremark is the No. 1 provider of prescriptions in the U.S. and the largest employer of pharmacists and nurse practitioners (advanced nurses who can write some prescriptions). About 75% of the U.S. population lives within three miles of a CVS store.

And CVS Caremark is just starting to see cost savings and operating efficiencies from multiple mergers it has completed since 2006. This streamlining promises to save $1 billion cumulatively through 2015.

CVS pays a small cash dividend and buys back stock. I also expect the company to increase the dividend as cash flows improve through merger efficiencies.

NO. 8: ABBVIE (NYSE: ABBV)

AbbVie Inc. (NYSE: ABBV) is a spinoff from the pharmaceutical and health-care giant Abbott Laboratories. Previously, Abbott was split into five segments: pharmaceutical, diagnostic, nutritional, vascular, and diabetes and eye care. In 2013, Abbott spun off AbbVie – the pharmaceutical segment. And it's been a success.

In many of its segments, AbbVie sells the leading drug, including Synthroid, a synthetic thyroid substitute, and Lupron for prostate cancer. Another well-known AbbVie drug is Humira, an antibody for autoimmune diseases, like rheumatoid arthritis.

Despite already selling leading drugs, AbbVie is working to introduce new drugs into the market. Currently, the company has more than 20 Phase II and III clinical programs. And it's not just working in the U.S. AbbVie sells products in more than 170 countries. The company's research centers are spread across the globe.

Its increasing global reach and drug pipeline is helping improve revenues. Total revenues rose from $17.4 billion in 2011 to nearly $18.4 billion in 2012. AbbVie is cheap compared to competitors. Right now, AbbVie is trading at a price-to-earnings ratio of 17x, lower than the industry's average ratio of 21.2x. And the company is rewarding shareholders with a dividend of 3.3%.

NO. 9: JOHNSON & JOHNSON (NYSE: JNJ)

One of my favorite companies in the world is **Johnson & Johnson (NYSE: JNJ)**. A leader in health care, JNJ's diversified business model ensures steady earnings. The company's three divisions include pharmaceutical (37.5%

of sales), medical devices and diagnostics (39.6%), and consumer segment (22.9%). The company has more than 250 operating companies globally.

And most important, JNJ plowed back nearly $37 billion into research and development from 2008-2012. This means its pipeline of new products, drugs, and ideas is full. In 2011 alone, the government approved five new JNJ drugs. This means buying JNJ is like buying a biotech hedge fund with inside information to hundreds of markets.

And JNJ is not shy about buying businesses, either. For example, it bought out the vaccine maker Crucell – but only after trying to form a joint venture with it in 2009. Once JNJ got a handle on the business and saw its potential... two years later, it bought the rest.

This company is one of the best-managed businesses trading today.

NO. 10: WALGREENS (NYSE: WAG)

Like its peer, CVS, the national drugstore chain **Walgreens (NYSE: WAG)** has been a nearly bulletproof operation that consistently rewards shareholders. It regularly increases its dividend and buys back shares.

As the Baby Boom generation ages... it'll be spending more and more on health care... and filling more and more prescriptions at their nearest drugstore...

And unlike book stores that have gone out of business because books can so easily be purchased online... many drugs are not cost effectively managed through the mail. And customers with acute needs will go to the store and pick up the drugs in person, rather than wait even a day for a shipment.

Walgreens is a popular place to find cheap deals on generic medications. And thanks to a 2013 deal with AmerisourceBergen – a pharmaceutical wholesaler – Walgreens can continue to sell prescription medications for low prices.

NO. 11: UNITED TECHNOLOGIES CORP. (NYSE: UTX)

United Technologies Corp. (NYSE: UTX) is a true industrial conglomerate. It has multiple businesses in multiple segments of the global economy.

It makes products as diverse as Carrier heating and cooling systems, Otis elevators, and Sikorsky helicopters. Several other segments make products for aerospace, food processing, and mining sectors. One division, UTC Power, is developing "environmentally advanced" fuel-cell and power products.

The company purchased Goodrich Corp. – a Charlotte, North Carolina-based aerospace company – for a little more than $18 billion. Goodrich is a leader in aviation products, including interiors, landing gears, and integrated electronic systems controls. This fits well since UTX also is a major aviation-equipment supplier.

In 2013, this company raised its dividend more than 9.7%, from $0.535 a share per quarter to $0.59. With little debt and steady cash flows, I expect dividend increases to continue.

NO. 12: WELLS FARGO (NYSE: WFC)

Wells Fargo (NYSE: WFC) is a California-based bank that provides corporate, commercial, and retail banking around the United States. Wells Fargo was among the financial institutions that accepted a bailout in 2008 from the federal Troubled Asset Relief Program (TARP)... as most big banks did.

The legendary head of Berkshire Hathaway, Warren Buffett is a WFC shareholder and loves the stock. This is another good sign for us as investors – to be right alongside one of the all-time best investors in history.

The most interesting measurement to watch in banks is the book value... Book value is what's left over after you take all the assets and subtract the liabilities. And Wells Fargo's book value has been growing.

But relative to WFC's share price, it is undervalued by historical standards. WFC's average price-to-book-value (P/BV) ratio for the past 30 years is 1.86x. I'd look to getting into this company when it trades for less than its average book value.

Given the slow comeback of the U.S. economy and the improving business cycle in the Western world, I look for U.S. banking stocks to improve over the next three years.

NO. 13: ORACLE CORP. (NASDAQ: ORCL)

Oracle Corp. (Nasdaq: ORCL) is a technology company that provides database services and software to more than 380,000 companies... including *all 100 members* of the Fortune 100 (the annual listing of the largest American businesses by gross revenue).

That's one of the most attractive features of investing in Oracle. Its products are everywhere. And that gives the company long-term loyalty. It's costly for Oracle clients to switch databases and software. You don't want to do it unless you're having major glitches. So Oracle is everywhere... and growing sensibly.

ORCL has positioned itself to be a key player in the next great technology move into the so-called "cloud." This is where businesses (and individuals) store their data, software, and systems offsite and access them via the Internet.

Given the comeback of the U.S. economy and the slowly improving global business cycles in Europe and South America, I look for U.S. technology stocks to quietly improve over the next three years. And this means businesses like Microsoft, Intel, and ORCL will reward shareholders.

NO. 14: COCA-COLA (NYSE: KO)

Coca-Cola (NYSE: KO) is one of the world's most recognized brands. Atlanta pharmacist John Pemberton founded Coca-Cola in 1886. Today, KO is still creating some of the world's most popular drinks.

It's the leader in beverages, offering an incredible array of 3,500 products (including carbonated drinks like Coca-Cola, juices like Minute Maid, and sports drinks like Powerade). KO sells beverages in more than 200 countries and employs more than 146,200 people worldwide.

Despite its industry leadership, Coca-Cola continues to grow. Its Coca-Cola Zero beverage grew 5% in volume in 2012 (it was originally introduced in 2005). And the company keeps expanding globally in places like Japan and Myanmar.

KO maintains a strong cash position and has rewarded shareholders through decades of dividend increases.

NO. 15: 3M CO. (NYSE: MMM)

Originally the Minnesota Mining and Manufacturing Company, five businessmen founded **3M Co. (NYSE: MMM)** to mine corundum for making sandpaper. For decades, it thrived on making abrasive products for the then-thriving car industry in Detroit. The company's first big mass market product came in 1925: masking tape. That quickly led to the brand of Scotch tape we know so well.

Today, the company is a well-diversified technology company... It makes abrasives, adhesives, filters, drug delivery systems, cleaning products, and even the granules for roofing shingles. This broad array of products results from 3M's long-standing philosophy that nourishes new ideas: Management encourages cross-division sharing and "bootlegging" of each other's ideas to create new products.

3M operates in more than 65 countries, with about two-thirds of sales coming from outside the United States. I like companies with large global footprints, because it spreads the economic risk. Other countries might be growing, while the U.S. is slowing... and vice versa.

NO. 16: MCDONALD'S (NYSE: MCD)

McDonald's (NYSE: MCD) is a global retail food-service empire. It's the world's largest fast-food retailer. Founded by Ray Kroc, McDonald's franchises and owns more than 33,000 restaurants in 119 countries, serving 68 million people per day. Wendy's – the second-largest burger chain in the U.S. and one of McDonald's closest competitors – has only 6,500 franchises worldwide. It's clear that McDonald's completely dominates its market.

McDonald's is practically printing money... Its double-digit profit margins resemble those of a high-technology company, rather than the narrow margins you'd expect of a burger joint.

In 2012, the company had more than $27 billion in revenues. Excluding a slight revenue decrease in 2009 (during the recession), McDonald's has served up steadily increasing revenues for the past 40 years.

It started paying a dividend 36 years ago in 1976 and has raised the payout every year since then... including through the worst recession since the 1930s. The company has a long history of rewarding shareholders with dividends and buybacks.

NO. 17: EXXONMOBIL (NYSE: XOM)

ExxonMobil (NYSE: XOM) is one of the world's leaders in energy exploration and production. It's the largest publicly traded oil and gas company in the world and among the world's most valuable companies, with a market cap of more than $408 billion.

The modern-day descendent of Standard Oil... Exxon has been minting money for generations and will continue to do so for generations. XOM may be the all-time greatest allocator of capital. It bought natural-gas properties when gas was at all-time lows and before others started bidding up the land...

XOM maintains a disciplined approach to investing its cash. The company invests for the long term and often reevaluates its investments to make sure they're profitable. This leader of energy production makes money year after year (and gives it back to shareholders through dividends and share buy backs).

ExxonMobil is the kind of stock you buy that lets you sleep well at night... You know you're going to keep earning a safe, solid dividend for years to come.

NO. 18: V.F. CORP. (NYSE: VFC)

Companies that offer lifetime guarantees on their products make me a loyal and lifetime customer. Case in point, **V.F. Corp. (NYSE: VFC)**.

You may not recognize the company's name... but it makes several of my favorite brands of clothing and outdoor gear: Wrangler jeans, North Face, Eagle Creek, and Eastpak. These names are well-known to many consumers.

VFC's product quality is unmatched, and its reputation for standing behind its stuff is amazing. Over the past 25 years, I have bought a few Eagle Creek products (travel bags and backpacks). When something would go wrong – say a broken zipper – a quick mailing to the company soon brought me either a fixed bag or a new version of the product. Because of that no-questions-asked/ lifetime guarantee, I regularly give Eagle Creek products as gifts...

Plus, this is a company that should grow globally during this improving business cycle. I expect to see increasing demand for high-quality products from Chinese and South American consumers... VFC has the lines and quality to meet that demand.

NO. 19: AUTOMATIC DATA PROCESSING (NASDAQ: ADP)

Automatic Data Processing (Nasdaq: ADP) is the "King of Payroll." It provides software and services to administer payroll, tax compliance, benefits, health insurance management, and more. No customer accounts for more than 2% of its revenues, which means it's well-diversified.

ADP is everywhere. It serves 555,000 clients. More than 90% of its revenues come from "recurring business," which means its clients stick around for a long, long time... and rarely leave. This is a tremendous feat.

ADP is a financial treasure. It holds little debt when compared with its cash hoard. If interest rates tick up as economies grow and lending increases, each 1% increase in interest rates could add nearly $280 million to its cash flow.

ADP has to hold on to a lot of cash. Its business is based on transferring cash from employers to employees, so it must remain liquid. Interest it earns on that cash hoard could add substantially to earnings if interest rates rise.

ADP operates in 63 countries. And 330 multinational companies (representing 52,000 employees) use its small-business product ADP Streamline. Nearly 100 clients (representing 750,000 workers) are contracted for ADP's larger business service, known as GlobalView. We love companies with this sort of international profile.

NO. 20: CHEVRON (NYSE: CVX)

Chevron (NYSE: CVX) is a behemoth... It's the third-largest oil and gas business in the world. It's also what's known as a "vertically integrated business." This means it owns the equipment to explore for oil and gas, the reserves of the resources, the pipes to extract them, the trucks and pipes to transport them, the plants to process and refine them, and the stations to deliver them.

Chevron controls the entire process of taking oil from the ground and turning it into gas in your tank. So its profits rise when prices of oil and gas go up. It does not have to pay any middlemen. If you tracked CVX earnings versus crude oil prices, you'd see how they move in tandem. CVX is a near-perfect hedge for rising energy prices.

One challenge for integrated oil companies is the need to regularly replenish their sources of energy. CVX is one of the best at doing so. Over the past 10 years, it has replaced 100% of its oil and gas reserves.

CVX has a growing stake in natural gas, should higher oil prices make "natty" more attractive than oil. It plans to add 30 trillion-40 trillion metric cubic feet of gas to its "proved reserves" this year. It does business in 180 countries, producing oil in places like the Philippines, Russia, Canada, and Brazil.

NO. 21: COLGATE-PALMOLIVE (NYSE: CL)

Colgate-Palmolive (NYSE: CL) was originally founded in 1806... William Colgate first started the company in New York City making and selling starches, soaps, and candles.

Today, it's a world leader in consumer goods. CL's products

are divided into four categories – Oral Care, Personal Care, Pet Nutrition, and Home Care. It sells its products in just about every country in the world with the help of 38,000 employees. Two of its most well-known products are its namesake Colgate toothpaste and Palmolive dish soap. Colgate is the No. 1 toothpaste in 146 countries – including the U.S., UK, and China. And CL's pet productions – including foods like Science Diet – control the market for vet recommendations worldwide.

This company knows how to make money... Sales increased from $15.3 billion in 2009 to $17.5 billion in 2013. And it's well-diversified. Of its sales, 80% come from outside the U.S., and 50% of revenues are from emerging markets...

With all the cash it generates, CL should have no problem continuing its dividend payments (as it has done for the last 117 years).

NO. 22: TARGET CORP. (NYSE: TGT)

In 1962, the first Target store opened in Roseville, Minnesota. What first was a small discount retailer has become one of the biggest major retail stores in the U.S. Today, **Target Corp. (NYSE: TGT)** sells just about everything... from food to furniture to every day personal items. You can also find a pharmacy and optical center in many stores.

As of 2009, Target operates stores in 49 states (the only exception is Vermont). And the company began expanding into Canada in 2013. It expects to open up to 200 stores coast-to-coast in the coming years.

These expansions are showing in the company's sales. In 2011, Target had record high sales of $68.5 billion and total revenues have increased from $63 billion in 2007 to almost $70 billion in 2013.

Target's also known for being generous with shareholders... It pays a steady dividend and has bought back billions of dollars in shares. I expect Target to continue to reward investors as it continues expanding.

NO. 23: HORMEL FOODS (NYSE: HRL)

Founded by George A. Hormel in 1891 as a meat-packing company outside Austin, Minnesota... **Hormel Foods (NYSE: HRL)** today is a name synonymous with packaged meat.

HRL is split into five business segments: grocery products, refrigerated products, Jennie-O Turkey Store, specialty foods, and international foods. Its range of products includes microwave meals, nutritional drinks, and grilling sauces. One of Hormel's best-known products – SPAM – hasn't changed much since it was first introduced in 1937...

And its products are global. In addition to being sold in all 50 states, HRL exports its goods to 40 countries.

Hormel's biggest business by far is the refrigerated foods, which accounted for 53% of net sales in 2012. In 2012, all five business segments saw an increase in sales, giving Hormel a record $8.2 billion in sales.

Hormel has enough cash to cover its little debt. But HRL doesn't just let cash sit around. Over the past five years, HRL has grown its dividend 12% annually... It's risen from $0.30 in 2007 to $0.80 in 2014.

NO. 24: THE CLOROX COMPANY
(NYSE: CLX)

The Clorox Company (NYSE: CLX) is a massive $9 billion consumer goods company. When you buy cleaning supplies or laundry detergent, there's a good chance you're buying a Clorox product.

When Clorox was founded in 1913, the company only made industrial-strength bleach using salt from the San Francisco Bay. Today, the company is split into four segments: cleaning, household, lifestyle, and international. And many of its brands from these segments are No. 1 in their markets. Several of its market-dominating brands include Brita water filters, Burt's Bee personal care products, and Clorox disinfecting wipes. Of all its products, 90% of Clorox's brands are either No. 1 or 2 in their markets.

Clorox sells its products in more than 100 countries and employs 8,100 worldwide. In the past two years, Clorox has made three big acquisitions – Caltech Industries (a hospital germicide and disinfectant manufacturer), and Aplicare and Healthlink, which make infection-control products for the health care industry (like antiseptics and antibacterial soaps).

From 2007 to 2013, CLX doubled its dividend – from $1.20 to $2.84 per share. And it can afford to... Net sales rose from $4.9 billion in 2008 to $5.6 billion in 2013 (during one of the toughest economic times the U.S. has faced).

This is what we look for... a company that keeps making money and keeps paying shareholders even in tough times.

NO. 25: THE WALT DISNEY COMPANY
(NYSE: DIS)

The Walt Disney Company (NYSE: DIS) first started as The Disney Brothers Studio in 1923. Thirty-two years later, Disney's founder, Walt Disney, opened Disneyland – the company's first theme park – in Anaheim, California. Since then, Disney has become one of the global leaders in entertainment.

Disney makes movies, toys, music, video games... It's the majority owner of major television companies like ABC and ESPN... And it has theme parks in California, Florida, France, Japan, and China.

2013 was another record year for Disney... Net income rose to $6.1 billion, a 27% increase from 2011. And revenues increased 10% from 2011 to $45 billion. Both numbers are record highs in the company's long history. Much of this can be attributed to two of Disney's recent acquisitions – Pixar Animation Studios and Marvel Entertainment. It also reflects the success of hit movies *Brave* and *Wreck-It Ralph*.

Thanks to these record sales and revenues, Disney has begun increasing its dividend again. From 2007 to 2009, Disney's dividend stayed at $0.35 per share. But it increased to $0.40 in 2010, $0.60 in 2011, and hit $0.86 in 2013. And with several highly anticipated movies releasing, theme park expansions, and its acquisition of Lucasfilm, I wouldn't be surprised to see more increases in the coming years.

FREQUENTLY ASKED QUESTIONS

– APPENDIX II –

I've been advising investors on option-selling strategies for many years. Here are some of the questions that come up over and over.

OPTIONS TRADING Q&A

QUESTION: Where can you find the prices options?

DOC EIFRIG ANSWER: You can find 15-minute delayed data on Yahoo Finance. Go to finance.yahoo.com. In the "Enter Symbol" box, enter the ticker of the stock you'd like to find options for. Once you pull up the main page for that stock, look along the left-hand side under "QUOTES." You'll find a link for "Options."

You should also be able to look up option prices on your broker's website, though it may display the data differently. Call your broker's customer service line for help.

QUESTION: When I look up option prices, I see bid and ask amounts. How do I reconcile those to what options I want to trade?

DOC EIFRIG ANSWER: This "bid" amount is the highest price option buyers are currently willing to pay. The "ask" amount is the lowest price option sellers are currently willing to accept.

Select your expiration month along the top. You'll see the calls at various strike prices. Scroll down to see the puts at various strike prices.

QUESTION: If I want to do a covered call trade, I know I have to own the stock first. But rather than do two separate transactions – buying the stock and then selling the call in a separate transaction (and paying a second commission) – can it be done as one transaction? If so, how would you put in this type of trade on an on-line broker system?

DOC EIFRIG ANSWER: Yes, you should be able to make a covered call trade – buy the stock and sell the call – in one transaction. Give your broker's customer service line a call. They'll be happy to walk you through entering the trade online. Just make sure they're not placing the order for you. That often costs extra.

QUESTION: When I try to sell options, I am presented with the option to "Sell to Open" or "Sell to Close." Can you advise me on the proper selection so I can execute the strategy correctly?

DOC EIFRIG ANSWER: When you begin (or "open") a covered call or naked put trade, you're selling the option. So you want to select "sell to open" on those options. If you want to exit the trade before expiration, you'll have to buy back those options. In that case, you'd "buy to close."

QUESTION: What does it mean to exercise an option?

DOC EIFRIG ANSWER: When someone owns an option – when he "buys to open" a call or put – he can exercise the option at will. In the case of a call, that means he can buy shares at the strike price. He can buy 100 shares for every call option contract he bought. With a put, he can sell the stock to you at the strike price.

If you're selling options, the trader who bought the option is allowed to exercise that option at any point until the option expires. That means you might be forced to sell shares at the strike price (if you sold a covered call).

Bear in mind, the option owner would be stupid to exercise the option when the share price is below the strike price (he could just go out and buy new shares on the open market for less). So you can expect the option owner to exercise the option only if the share price is higher than the strike price on expiration day.

QUESTION: Through my broker, I have four choices for "duration." They are "Day," "Good Till Canceled," "Immediate or Cancel," and "Fill or Kill." I also have a box I can check for "All or None." Can you explain the differences and/or benefits of the choices?

DOC EIFRIG ANSWER: If you enter "day," your order will last until it gets filled or until the market closes for the day. "Good till canceled" (GTC) means your order will stay open until it gets filled or you cancel it.

"Immediate or Cancel" means you want all or part of the trade to be filled right away. Any part of the trade that's not filled will be canceled. "Fill or kill" is similar, except it means you want the whole order to be filled immediately or cancelled entirely. "All or none" means you either want the whole order filled by the close of the market or canceled.

For most traders, the "day" or "good till canceled" choices make sense. Use "good till canceled" if you're willing to wait for a great price and are OK missing the trade if you never get it. Using the "day" choice will ensure you never have an old, forgotten order floating around.

A great, free resource when you run into jargon like this is Investopedia. It offers short, common-sense definitions.

QUESTION: Suppose a stock I sold calls against soars by the time of expiration? If I had been prescient enough to just buy the shares and hold them for the same period of time, I could have sold out and made a much higher gain. By selling the option, then, haven't I actually lost money?

DOC EIFRIG ANSWER: Obviously, you haven't lost a thing. You've made a stellar trade. Your point, of course, is that you could have made an even better trade.

If you believe a stock is going to skyrocket, you shouldn't sell calls against your shares. You'll cap your gains. Instead, you should buy it.

But if you like the idea of collecting "instant income" and giving yourself a large margin of safety – and if you can let go of the idea of the "perfect trade" – then writing covered calls on high-quality companies is a great strategy.

QUESTION: If you sell to open a covered call and already own the same or greater number of shares as covered by the number of contracts you sell – in the same account – do you still have to purchase more shares at the time of your execution?

DOC EIFRIG ANSWER: If you already own shares, you can just sell a call against them. You don't need to buy more shares before you sell the call.

QUESTION: Every covered call trade I've made looks like it's losing money. But I still have the premium I received, plus I'll get more for the stock than I paid for it if I'm called away. For instance, I sold six Microsoft August $29 call contracts for $1.35. By my calculations, I have made $810. But my broker is reporting a loss of $232. How can that be?

DOC EIFRIG ANSWER: Your broker is showing you what your returns would be on the option portion of your covered call trade if you closed the trade out today.

The calls you sold for $1.35 are now trading for about $1.75. If you were to buy back the call, you'd pay $0.40 more than you received, for a total "loss" of about $240 ($0.40 times 100 per contract times six).

A more useful way to think about your return on the option part of your trade – as you point out – is to consider the premium you received as income. You pocketed $810 ($1.35 times 100 per contract times six). The current price of the option is immaterial because you get to keep that $810 no matter what.

To calculate your potential gains on the "whole" trade – the option and the stock – you need to factor in what you paid to buy shares.

QUESTION: If the price of the underlying stock advances high enough beyond the strike price on a covered call trade, do you recommend that we "buy back" the call? If so, what are the costs?

DOC EIFRIG ANSWER: When you're selling options, time is on your side. All things equal, your best bet is to wait while the "time value" of the call erodes.

Now... if the share price of the stock you sold calls on skyrockets, you might kick yourself for missing out on those capital gains and settling for the option premium... but you shouldn't. You're in it for the income, and you achieved your goals.

In this situation, there's no point in buying back the call. It will have increased about $1 for every $1 the share price moved up. There's nothing to gain by buying it back. Wait for your shares to get called away, and keep an eye out for the next opportunity.

QUESTION: If I sell a covered call and an action is required on my part to sell a stock, will I be notified by someone on what I need to do and when? Also, if a sell is required, I assume I will pay a commission on the transaction in addition to the option fees, correct?

DOC EIFRIG ANSWER: If you sell a covered call and shares end up over the strike price on option-expiration day, your broker will automatically sell your shares... and will charge you a commission.

At TDAmeritrade, that commission is about double the normal fee. But that'll vary from broker to broker.

QUESTION: What if I sell a covered call on Wal-Mart with a strike price of $70 and suddenly Wal-Mart goes to $80? Won't I lose money if I'm forced to sell something $10 below its market price? If so, is there a stop loss strategy that I should use when SELLING covered calls?

DOC EIFRIG ANSWER: Rule No. 1 for selling covered calls is this: Never sell a covered call on a stock you're not willing to sell. When you're making covered call trades, you're giving up potential gains beyond the strike price in exchange for immediate income.

If you believe a stock is going to zoom hundreds of percent higher, you don't want to cap your gains by selling covered calls. But if you're in it for the income, whether the stock goes to $80 or $100 shouldn't matter. You've pocketed your gains.

QUESTION: If you sell a $65 covered call on Wal-Mart, are you required to sell before the expiration date if Wal-Mart closes above $65 at any time between now and then?

DOC EIFRIG ANSWER: If the trader who bought your call wants to "exercise" his option early, he can force you to sell shares at any time after you've sold your covered call.

If he does so "early" – before the expiration date – it's to your benefit. You've collected the full premium from the call in less time than you expected. You can use that capital to generate even more income.

QUESTION: Wouldn't it make us more income to sell a call each month, rather than sell one call with an expiration date several months out?

DOC EIFRIG ANSWER: When you're selling options, the further out in time you go, the more total income you collect... But the less income you get per unit of time. So you're right that at the end of the year, you might end up with more income if you sell a call every month rather than selling a call every two or three months.

But the more you trade, the more fees you incur. And because one-month options carry lower premiums, you'll end up sending a higher percentage of your premium right back to your broker. That's why we usually prefer to go out a couple months or more when we're selecting an expiration date.

QUESTION: How is selling a put the same as selling a covered call?

DOC EIFRIG ANSWER: Selling a covered call is mathematically identical to selling a put – based on the capital at risk. It's just a different way to put on the same trade.

The only difference is a put requires less cash upfront. For puts, you have to put up "margin," usually about 20% of the money you would be obligated to pay if the option is executed against you. With a covered call, you have to buy shares in the stock.

When you see a difference in gains between puts and calls, this reflects the initial capital outlay. But remember... the put may be obligate you to pay the other 80% if the stock is put to you... That's a real obligation. And when you factor that in, your gains are the same.

Let's use another Intel trade from August 2011 as an example...

The stock was trading for around $19.33. We sold a put with a $19 strike price for $0.47. So we were agreeing to buy the stock for a net cost basis of $18.53 per share ($19 minus $0.47) if the option expired with the stock trading for less than $19.

I also provided a covered call option. In that case, we bought the stock for $19.47 and sold a call with a $19 strike price for $0.98.

So in both cases, we were betting Intel would trade for more than $19 by option expiration in September.

The covered call position required an initial outlay of $1,849 – the cost of 100 shares of stock minus the premium we received for selling the call.

In the put trade, the initial capital outlay was $380 – a margin requirement of 20% of what we would have to pay to buy 100 shares at $19 apiece. But if we were forced to buy the stock, our capital outlay would jump to $1,853... virtually the same as our call strategy (a $4 difference).

Again, it's just a different way to get into the same trade. And in both cases, you're collecting more income and taking on less risk than you would with an outright stock purchase.

QUESTION: What is the benefit of having to deposit only 20%? It seems more like an accounting fiction. Is the benefit of 20% margin only realized if the stock is not put to me?

DOC EIFRIG ANSWER: The benefit is that you can have the other 80% of your potential obligation sitting in cash elsewhere earning a little more money (albeit nearly nothing these days).

QUESTION: If you sell a put option on a stock and that stock is acquired by another company before expiration, how is this situation resolved?

DOC EIFRIG ANSWER: Unless the stock is put to you by the buyer of the put, you won't do anything. Remember... the option to exercise is with the buyer, not you, the seller.

If the company is acquired, there's no more stock to sell back to you once the deal closes. And in most cases, the stock runs up above the strike once deal is announced... again, letting you pocket the money.

QUESTION: Does selling puts without owning the stock still entitles us to dividends as if we own the stock?

DOC EIFRIG ANSWER: No. When we're selling uncovered puts, we're not holding the stock. So, we aren't paid dividends. If you sell covered calls, you would receive dividends because you're holding the stock.

And even though the math is nearly identical between a naked put and a covered call, the option prices take the dividends into account.

ANATOMY OF AN OPTION AND GLOSSARY OF TERMS

– APPENDIX III –

Every option follows a conventional naming system... and that name includes all the key pieces of data you need to trade that option. Every stock name includes the stock symbol for the underlying, the expiration date, the strike price and whether it's a call or put.

Options (like stocks) also have a unique "ticker" assigned to them. Those tickers also include all the critical identifying data: Underlying stock symbol; expiration year, month, and day; whether it's a put or call; and the strike price.

The option name and ticker typically look something like this, depending on the platform. Here's one from Yahoo Finance...

Underlying Asset   Strike Price   Symbol   Exp. Month   Strike Price

MSFT Apr 2014 30.000 call (MSFT140419C00030000)

Expiration Month   Call or Put   Exp. Year   Exp. Day   Call or Put

GLOSSARY OF TERMS

Underlying Instrument: The stock, stock index, or any other financial instrument that the option-buyer has the right to buy and sell.

Premium: The price of the option.

Expiration Date: Options usually expire on the third Friday of the month.

Exercise: A trader who has bought on option can exercise the right to buy (in the case of a call) or sell (in the case of a put) the underlying instrument at the strike price. *Retirement Trader* readers will rarely have to worry about exercising an option... The right to exercise an option is held by the buyer... And we're typically sellers options of puts and calls.

Strike Price: The price at which you can "exercise" your option. This price is based on the underlying instrument. Call-option buyers have the right to buy the underlying instrument at the strike price. Put-option buyers have the right to sell at the strike price.

In the Money: Calls are "in the money" if the price of the underlying instrument is HIGHER than the strike price. Puts are "in the money" if the price of the underlying instrument is LOWER than the strike price. (A put with a $20 strike price is "in the money" by $1 with the stock at $19.)

At the Money: When the price of the underlying instrument is identical to the strike price. Same for both puts and calls.

Out of the Money: Calls are "out of the money" if the price of the underlying instrument is LOWER than the strike price. Puts are "out of the money" if the price of the underlying instrument is HIGHER than the strike price. (A crude-oil call with a strike price of $25 is "out of the money" if crude is at $20.)

Symbol: The basic parts of an option symbol are: Stock Symbol + Expiration Year + Expiration Month + Expiration Day + Call/Put Indicator + Strike price. You can see how this works in the earlier example.

In his *Retirement Trader* advisory, Dr. Eifrig used the techniques described in this book to compile an incredible track record of success. Over a period of more than three years, he closed an unprecedented 136 consecutive positions for gains.

If you'd like to subscribe to *Retirement Trader* and receive regular trading recommendations from Dr. Eifrig, please visit:

http://stansberryresearch.com/products/Retirement-Trader/

82655683R00082

Made in the USA
Middletown, DE
04 August 2018